UNDERSTANDING APARTHEID

Learner's Book

OXFORD
UNIVERSITY PRESS

APARTHEID MUSEUM

OXFORD
UNIVERSITY PRESS

Southern Africa

Oxford University Press Southern Africa (Pty) Ltd

Vasco Boulevard, Goodwood, Cape Town, Republic of South Africa
P O Box 12119, N1 City, 7463, Cape Town, Republic of South Africa

Oxford University Press Southern Africa (Pty) Ltd is a wholly-owned subsidiary of
Oxford University Press, Great Clarendon Street, Oxford OX2 6DP.

The Press, a department of the University of Oxford, furthers the University's objective of
excellence in research, scholarship, and education by publishing worldwide in

Oxford New York

Auckland Dar es Salaam Hong Kong Karachi
Kuala Lumpur Madrid Melbourne Mexico City Nairobi
New Delhi Shanghai Taipei Toronto

With offices in

Argentina Austria Brazil Chile Czech Republic France Greece
Guatemala Hungary Italy Japan Poland Portugal Singapore South Korea
Switzerland Turkey Ukraine Vietnam

Oxford is a registered trade mark of Oxford University Press
in the UK and in certain other countries

Published in South Africa
by Oxford University Press Southern Africa (Pty) Ltd, Cape Town

Understanding Apartheid Learner's Book
ISBN 0 19 576617 2 (10-digit, current)
ISBN 978 0 19 576617 2 (13-digit, from 2007)

© Apartheid Museum

The moral rights of the author have been asserted
Database right Oxford University Press Southern Africa (Pty) Ltd (maker)

First published 2006

Publisher: Claudia Bickford-Smith
Senior Editor: Carolynne Lengfeld
Editor: Sara Pienaar
Designer: Lauren Rycroft, Flame Design
Cover Design: Lauren Rycroft, Flame Design
Typesetter: Flame Design

Set in 8,5 pt on 11 pt on CorporateS-Regular by Flame Design
Printed by Creda Communications

This book grew out of a partnership between the Gauteng Department of Education (GDE) and the Apartheid Museum in 2003. The Museum would like to thank the GDE, and especially Tom Waspe, Rae Davids and Ivor Hoff.

Thanks to Michelle Friedman, Professor Philip Bonner and Gail Behrmann for their important contributions. Thanks also to Claudia Bickford-Smith and Carolynne Lengfeld of Oxford University Press, as well as editors Sara Pienaar and Mary Monteith. The various organizations which have served on the Museum's Education Committee also helped to shape this project. They included the Foundation for Tolerance Education, SADTU, EISA, SAHRC and the CSVR. We would also like to acknowledge the generous grant from the C.S. Mott Foundation which allows us to distribute *Understanding Apartheid* to teachers visiting the Apartheid Museum for a nominal fee.

Finally, the Museum would like to recognize the crucial role played by our Education Manager, Emilia Potenza. Her commitment to teaching young people about apartheid was the driving force behind this project.

Christopher Till
Director
Apartheid Museum

CHARLES STEWART
MOTT FOUNDATION

CONTENTS

How to use this book

Understanding Apartheid is divided into five chapters. Each chapter focuses on a different aspect of apartheid. The content is dealt with within the context of the current school senior and FET phase curricula and is suitable for both home language and additional language learners.

The table below shows how this book integrates with the History Senior Phase and FET band curricula.

GRADE 8	GRADE 9	GRADE 11	GRADE 12
Industrialization in South Africa: diamonds and gold, and changing work and lives in South Africa on the mines, the land and the cities (including the 1913 Land Act).	Apartheid in South Africa: • Impact of World War Two • What was apartheid? • How did it affect peoples' lives? • Repression and resistance to apartheid in the 1950s (e.g. the Defiance Campaign, the Freedom Charter and popular culture). • Repression and the armed struggle in the 1960s. • Divide and rule: the role of the homelands. • Repression and the growth of mass democratic movements in the 1970s and 1980s: external and internal pressure. • Building a new identity in South Africa in the 1990s: pre-1994 negotiations, the first democratic elections and South Africa's Constitution.	How unique was apartheid in South Africa? • How was segregation a foundation for apartheid? • To what extent was apartheid in South Africa part of neo-colonialism in the post World War Two world (1948 – 1960)? • How did apartheid entrench ideas of race? • What was the nature of resistance to apartheid during these decades, and how was this resistance part of the wider resistance in the world to human rights abuses. • How has the South African past been publically represented in museums?	What forms of civil society protest emerged from the 1960s up to 1990? • The 1970s; The Black Consciousness Movement in South Africa. How did South Africa emerge as a democracy from the crises of the 1990s? • The crisis of apartheid in the 1980s. • The collapse of apartheid in South Africa – coming together of internal and external pressures. • How the crises were managed – conflict, compromise, negotiation, settlement, elections. • The government of national unity and the making of the Constitution. • New identities and the construction of heritage.

Understanding Apartheid has numerous features to make teaching and learning about this topic easy and interesting.

New words are highlighted in the text and explained fully in the page-by-page glossary.

An indication of where activities integrate with History Learning Outcomes and Assessment Standards in the Senior Phase and FET band.

Carefully selected visuals add value to the text and consolidate learning.

Activities provide a variety of accessible learning experiences that accommodate learners with varying learning styles.

A content feature shows how the content of this book links with the History Senior Phase and FET band curricula.

Guidelines for developing skills, helps learners to answer questions.

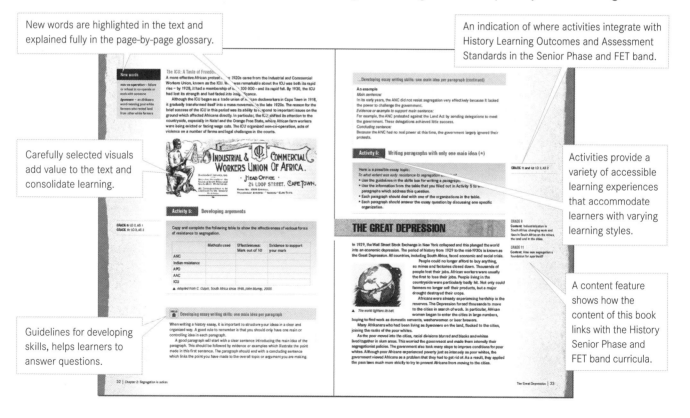

Assessment

 Assessment opportunities are provided for Grades 8, 9, 11 and 12 with more demanding activities highlighted by means of an asterisk (*).

Dear Learner

You have before you a history of apartheid – one of the first published for schools in South Africa. This book provides you with the opportunity to understand why our country suffered under this policy of racial discrimination.

The system of racial domination created deep and lasting wounds in our people and country. Many people will spend years, if not generations, recovering from that profound hurt. But the decades of oppression and brutality had another, unintended, effect. They produced leaders, people of extraordinary courage, wisdom and generosity. You will read about them in this book. They, and the ordinary men and women of this country, made the difference. Together they led the way out of oppression.

The unimaginable sacrifices of previous generations – their courage and suffering – can never be counted or repaid. But it is through understanding history and why events happened that we can all begin to move forward into a new era – the new South Africa in the twenty first century.

It is with ideas of sacrifice, freedom and responsibility in mind that the Nelson Mandela Foundation asks you to read this history and to engage with the important ideas of tolerance and forgiveness. We hope that your generation of South African youth will be known for its respect for and acceptance of one another, regardless of background, colour, creed or class, so that this country, beloved by us all, will flourish and continue to grow in its generosity of spirit.

NELSON MANDELA FOUNDATION

NELSON MANDELA
FOUNDATION
Living the Legacy

CHAPTER 1

THE ORIGINS OF APARTHEID

History itself is a **dynamic** subject and is constantly subject to change. By recovering and investigating some of the hidden stories of the past, we construct a new and broader understanding of human experience. It is therefore important to recognize that history is not a fixed body of information. Rather, it is a process of continually finding out and asking new questions about the past. As we gather more information from new sources, our view of history may change and with it, our understanding of the world we live in.

Studying history involves understanding the broader context of the period or events we are learning about. This helps us to make informed judgements about the usefulness and reliability of the source material available to us about these events.

GRADE 8 and 9
Content: The conservation and representation of South Africa's cultural heritage

GRADE 11
Content: How has the South African past been publicly represented in museums?

GRADE 12
Content: New identities and the construction of heritage

UNDERSTANDING APARTHEID

Apartheid – why study it?

Learning about apartheid is a difficult and challenging process. You will discover many painful truths about our country and develop an understanding of the darkness of our past. However, you will also gain an insight into the courage, determination and creativity of ordinary people who eventually defeated apartheid.

This book encourages you to go on a journey of understanding from the tortured history of South Africa's past to the hope for the future that the democratic elections of 1994 offered. On the way, you will encounter many different perspectives of the apartheid past, which will challenge your minds and touch your hearts.

The Apartheid Museum is a heritage site which was developed to commemorate and explain the atrocities of the apartheid past. Visitors to the museum are also encouraged to go on a personal journey of discovery through engaging with the exhibits, photographs and oral histories of people who lived through these experiences. This book follows a path similar to that taken by the Apartheid Museum and it uses many of the same resources to help you on your journey through our past.

MEMORY AND THE APARTHEID MUSEUM

▲ *The separate entrances to the Apartheid Museum.*

The separate entrances to the Apartheid Museum – one for 'whites', one for 'non-whites' – are a haunting reminder of our not-so-distant past, when blacks and whites were racially **segregated** in all aspects of their lives. This separation of the races was a daily reality, and one which brought great hardships for black South Africans. And yet today, not that many years after the death of apartheid, there are many young South Africans who do not know that this was how South Africans lived. Sadly, there are a growing number of young South Africans who do not care.

Milan Kundera, a Czech **dissident** and writer, recognizes the importance of remembering the past. "The struggle of [people] against power is the struggle of memory against forgetting." What Kundera means is that the past is always in danger of being controlled and manipulated by those in power.

In the past, the histories of ordinary South Africans were deliberately forgotten. South African museums housed exhibitions that related mainly to the rich and powerful, while the memories and experiences of ordinary people were regarded as irrelevant. The new approach to the study of history allows us to appreciate the lives of ordinary people and to honour their contribution to our society.

The Apartheid Museum aims to keep memory alive by presenting the story of apartheid and how it affected the lives of millions of ordinary South Africans.

"The overriding message is to show local and international visitors the **perilous** results of racial prejudice and how this, in the case of South Africa, caused enormous suffering and nearly destroyed the country," says John Kani, Chairman of the Board of the Apartheid Museum.

New words

dynamic – constantly moving or changing

segregated – separated and treated differently, in this case, because of their race

dissident – a person who opposes the established government

perilous – dangerous, full of risk

*History will remember
the ones who struggled unnoticed
as small and as many as the grains of sand
on our beautiful shores.*

▲ Sweet Freedom, *a song about Wilton and Irene Mkwayi by Jennifer Ferguson.*

Apartheid is an old story. You dwell on that, it just turns you sour.

Only through understanding what happened in the past, and how apartheid has hurt us as a people, can we begin to heal, and reconciliation can take place.

What's past is past. We need to move forward. The sooner the ugly memories of apartheid fade, the better.

By remembering what happened here in South Africa, we can try to make sure that this kind of thing never happens again.

The fact that we carry any knowledge of the past is not a matter of people constantly remembering: people remember because teachers and writers constantly seek to remind them.
*Professor Kader Asmal, MP,
Former Minister of Education*

We need to study apartheid in order to understand the problems we face as a society today.

GRADE 8: LO 3, AS 6
GRADE 9: LO 3, AS 4
GRADE 11 and 12: LO 4, AS 1

Where do you stand on this issue?
1. Have a class debate in which you look at the role of memory, the past, and the place of history in our lives.
2. Discuss this issue with your parents. What do they think about the past and the study of history? Do they have similar or different feelings to you?

New words

reconstructing – creating a description of something that happened using the facts that are known

collective memory – memories of what happened to a community which are shared by all its members, even if some of them were not present when the events took place

"The struggle of memory against forgetting"

Memory is about remembering and forgetting; it is about including and excluding events in the past; it is about **reconstructing** a new meaning of what happened; it is the key which unlocks the hidden voices and experiences of the past. It is for this reason that memory is an important theme of the Apartheid Museum. The Museum attempts to jolt our **collective memory** and to reconstruct aspects of our recent past in a reliable way.

As you enter the Museum, you are confronted with the figures of ordinary South Africans from a wide range of different walks of life. In the Museum, the fragile memories of these individuals and their families are contained in memory boxes. These are personal items chosen by the families, which represent valuable experiences in their past. They show us where they have come from, and what was important to them in their past.

▲ John Nkadimeng - son of Mahudu Nkadimeng, who came to work on the gold mines as a migrant labourer in the early 1900s – as pictured on the ramp of the Apartheid Museum.

▲ Prospero Bailey – grandson of Abe Bailey, a mine owner in early Johannesburg – as pictured on the ramp of the Apartheid Museum.

Below are the contents of the memory boxes belonging to the Nkadimeng and Bailey families. We have chosen to focus on the memory boxes of these two families because, later in the book, we examine the contribution of John Nkadimeng's father and Prospero Bailey's grandfather to the early history of Johannesburg.

◀ Prospero Bailey's father, Jim Bailey, founded Drum magazine which documented black culture and politics in the cities in the 1950s and 1960s. This magazine is an item in the memory box of the Bailey family.

▲ These clay pots and this calabash for drinking milk remind John Nkadimeng of his childhood in Sekhukhuneland. John was still very young when his father, Mahudu Nkadimeng, died.

Create your own memory box.
1. Choose two or three items that are particularly meaningful to you and your family or that represent aspects of your own history.
2. Write a brief explanation of why you chose each item.
3. Present your memory box to the class.
4. Is the class able to gain a sense of who you are and what was meaningful in your past, through your memory box? This should form the basis of a class discussion.

Note: You are dealing with sources of information about your own history. Treat these items with care.

GRADE 8: LO 3, AS 7
GRADE 9: LO 3, AS 4
GRADE 11: LO 4, AS 1
GRADE 12: LO 4, AS 3

EXPLAINING APARTHEID: DIFFERENT APPROACHES

GRADE 11
Content: Historiography and the origins of apartheid

How did apartheid come about?

The Apartheid Museum encourages visitors to ask the question: how did apartheid come about? The answer to this question is not simple, and has been the subject of heated debate amongst historians. The word apartheid means separation. The fact that the government of the day found it necessary to separate people suggests that there was a natural mixing of people at the time. The decision to separate groups of people on the basis of race was deliberate; it was not something that occurred naturally. Through the course of this book, we will explore why the apartheid government was determined to keep different races separate.

There are four broad interpretations or theories that try to explain apartheid.

Race and apartheid

Although it is impossible for us to talk about apartheid without referring to the issue of race, it is important to note that race is not a scientifically verifiable way of defining people. Race is something that is socially constructed in order to justify the superiority of one social group over another.

1. The Afrikaner Nationalist Approach

Afrikaner Nationalists believed in the superiority of the Afrikaner nation. They believed that their identity was 'God-given'. They feared that the Afrikaner's very existence was threatened by the mass of Africans that confronted them in South Africa; that the Afrikaner nation would be swamped and overcome if there was continued mixing of the races. Afrikaner Nationalist historians explain apartheid in 1948 as the consolidation of these beliefs through a range of laws that were passed to prevent the mixing of the races and to preserve this 'God-given' Afrikaner identity.

▲ Dr Hendrik Verwoerd was the prime minister of South Africa from 1958 to 1966 and is often given the title of the 'Architect of Apartheid'.

2. The Liberal Approach

Liberals believe in a society which upholds human rights and the **fundamental freedoms** of the individual. In an economic sense, they believe in the freedom of the market with minimal state interference. In trying to explain why apartheid arose, they emphasize the importance of race and argue that the idea of white **supremacy** played the most important role.

Liberals are opposed to racial **discrimination** and condemn apartheid as a form of racial hatred which dates back to very early struggles over the land. They deny that there were any economic benefits to be gained from apartheid and place the blame for apartheid on the National Party which came into power in 1948.

▲ *Big Business, which claimed to be liberal, benefited from segregation and apartheid policies which provided them with a source of cheap labour and greater profits. This cartoon suggests that Big Business was hypocritical. It portrays Big Business as a Pinocchio-like figure, whose nose grows longer with every lie he tells.*

3. The Radical Approach

▲ *Migrant workers provided the cheap, unskilled labour required by the gold mines on the Witwatersrand.*

Radical historians tend to focus on the economic and social development of South Africa. They examine **class differences** and the struggles that took place between the different classes to explain why South African society emerged as it did. They view apartheid as a continuation of the **segregationist policies** that were developed as a result of the labour needs of the gold mines.

These policies were established in order to create a large supply of cheap labour which was needed for the profitable extraction of gold through deep-level mining. To sustain this system of **exploitation**, radicals argue that the authorities could not allow black workers to become skilled, or to be permanent residents in the city. Nor could they be granted citizenship or any other rights that would enable them to challenge the system.

4. The Social History Approach

Social historians study the lives of ordinary people and the impact of their actions and thoughts on the course of history, rather than the lives of the rich and the powerful. This is often referred to as 'history from below'. Social historians make use of a range of different kinds of sources in order to reconstruct history, including oral interviews, fiction and poetry, songs and pictures, as well as more official sources. They see oral history as a particularly useful means of focusing on the voices of ordinary people, whose thoughts and ideas are usually not found in official sources, as they were not usually recorded.

In explaining apartheid, social historians examine the role played by ordinary people in resisting the growing restrictions placed upon them. This resistance often led policy makers to pass increasingly harsh laws in order to control them. It also shows how poorer people of all races initially mixed in the cities and highlights the fact that racial mixing was more natural than racial separation.

▲ *An ordinary family affected by the Depression in the 1930s.*

New words

fundamental freedoms – the right to vote, the right to a fair trial, freedom of speech, religion and the press

supremacy – a belief that one group is superior to all others, the highest in authority

discrimination – treating one person or group worse than others (in this case, because of their race)

class differences – according to radical thinkers, society is divided into different classes. The ruling class owns business and industry, and is therefore very powerful. The working class works for the ruling class and has little power. This imbalance of power often leads to conflict between these two classes.

segregationist policies – policies that promoted the separation of people and treated them differently according to their race

exploitation – the process whereby workers earn wages that are less than the value of their labour and goods they produce

Activity 3:	**Understanding different schools of thought (∗)**

GRADE 11: LO 2, AS 3

1. Identify the differences between these four approaches to understanding apartheid.
2. As you work through this book, see if you can identify which interpretation/s of apartheid are being presented by the people who produced it.

GRADE 8
Content: Industrialization in
South Africa: changing work and
lives in South Africa on the mines,
the land and in the cities

GRADE 11
Content: How unique was
apartheid South Africa – how
was segregation a foundation for
apartheid?

THE GLITTER OF GOLD: LAYING THE FOUNDATIONS OF APARTHEID

To understand the roots of apartheid, it is important to examine how South African society changed when gold was discovered on the Witwatersrand in 1886.

It is no accident that the Apartheid Museum was built at Gold Reef City, on the site of an old disused mine. The discovery of gold on the Witwatersrand was central to both South Africa's industrial development and to the politics of segregation. It was here, on the goldfields of the Rand, that the journeys of many people intersected.

Within a period of ten years of the discovery of gold, Johannesburg had developed into the largest city in South Africa. Prospectors, labourers, fortune hunters, shopkeepers and immigrants from all over the world flocked to the city. Residential areas were hastily constructed and, in the poorer sections, slums developed. Racial mixing became a feature of these slums. The policies of segregation, and later apartheid, were attempts to stop this racial mixing.

> "There can be no doubt that the historian ... will point to the period between the discovery of gold on the Witwatersrand and the establishment of the city of Johannesburg as a turning point in the history not only of Southern Africa but of the whole continent."
>
> R.V. Selope Thema, 1886-1955, leading newspaper editor, intellectual and African Nationalist.

▶ *Johannesburg in 1886 when gold was discovered.*

| Activity 4: | **Examining a photograph as an historical source (∗)** |

Photograph of Johannesburg, 1886
1. In the Apartheid Museum, a whole wall has been dedicated to the photograph above of Johannesburg in 1886. Why do you think the Museum has chosen to use such a large and dominant photograph of early Johannesburg?
2. What are the main features of this photograph?
3. Why do you think the photographer took this photograph? What was he trying to convey?
4. Do you think Selope Thema's comment about the importance of Johannesburg is a suitable quote to accompany this photograph?
5. What other caption could have been used for this photograph? Give a clear reason for your choice.

▶ *Johannesburg, looking east along the Reef in 1906, only twenty years after the discovery of gold.*

1. Compare the photograph of Johannesburg in 1906 with the one above it taken in 1886. List the main changes between 1886 and 1906 that you can see in the photographs.
2. Give two reasons why you think these changes took place.
3. What, for you, is the most surprising change to have taken place in the twenty years? Give a clear reason for your answer.
4. Provide a more interesting caption for this photograph of early Johannesburg in 1886 than the one provided here.

GRADE 8: LO 1, AS 2 and 3
GRADE 11: LO 1, AS 3

"*I am slowly being confirmed in my opinion that Johannesburg is Hell. Every man living for himself, every man fighting for gold, gold, gold and tramping down everything that stands in his way.*"

▲ Letter from Olive Schreiner to Miss Green, 25 January 1899.

JOURNEYS TO THE GOLDFIELDS

GRADE 8
Content: Industrialization in South Africa: changing work and lives in South Africa on the mines, the land and in the cities

GRADE 11
Content: How unique was apartheid South Africa – how was segregation a foundation for apartheid?

Let us consider the journeys to the goldfields of two people, Abe Bailey and Mahudu Nkadimeng, after gold was discovered in 1886. They represent the many thousands of people who came to Johannesburg to seek their fortunes – and in the process shaped the history of South Africa.

▲ Alfred Beit   ▲ Joseph Robinson   ▲ Abe Bailey   ▲ Cecil Rhodes   ▲ Julius Wernher

Abe Bailey, and the other **mining magnates** like Cecil John Rhodes, Alfred Beit, Julius Wernher and Joseph Robinson, were known as Randlords. They saw an opportunity to make large fortunes on the gold mines, and of course, many of them did. They were able to gain control of the gold mines with the capital (profits) they had made on the Kimberley diamond fields. They made themselves and the gold mines even stronger and wealthier by forming the Chamber of Mines to protect their interests.

However, these Randlords were confronted with three problems when it came to mining gold. The first was that the gold reserves were deep underground and deep-level mining was extremely expensive. Secondly, the gold-bearing ore (rock) was 'low-grade'. A lot of ore had to be dug out and then the gold had to be extracted from the ore. This was also expensive. Thirdly, the price of gold was internationally-fixed, which meant that the Randlords could not transfer their high production costs to consumers by charging them very high prices.

In order to make large profits in the mining industry, it was necessary to limit the cost of producing gold. A major area where costs could be cut was wages. The Randlords

New word

mining magnates – wealthy men who controlled the mining industry

believed that they could find a cheap source of labour by using black migrant labour. (The life of one migrant labourer, Mahudu Nkadimeng, will be examined later.)

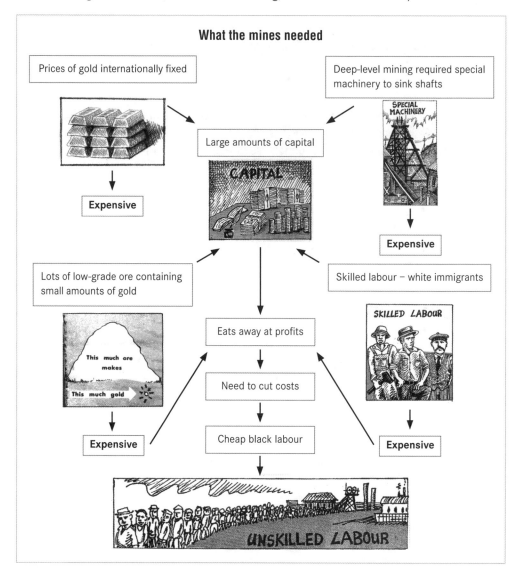

What the mines needed

Activity 6:   The needs of the gold mines

GRADE 8: LO 2, AS 2
GRADE 11: LO 2, AS 3

Study the above diagram and then answer these questions:
1. What is meant by the term 'capital'?
2. List four factors from the diagram which show that gold mining was an expensive enterprise.
3. Explain how the internationally-fixed gold price affected the ability of the Randlords to make profits.
4. In what way did deep-level mining make gold mining expensive?
5. How did the fact that the ore was low-grade contribute to the expense of mining gold on the Witwatersrand?
6. "The Witwatersrand deposits are at once the richest and the poorest in the world." Explain this statement made by the historian C.W. de Kiewiet in 1941. (*)
7. What is the difference between skilled labour and unskilled labour? (*)
8. Why do you think the use of white skilled labour was expensive? (*)
9. "The mines needed cheap black labour in order to survive." Write ten lines to explain this statement. (*)

Where was this source of cheap labour to come from?

During the late nineteenth century, the majority of Africans in South Africa worked as **independent peasant farmers**. Although they faced pressures from natural disasters and many had lost their land to white farmers, many African farmers made a successful living working on the land. As a result, they did not have to go and work for wages on the mines in order to make a living.

However, as deep-level mining increased, the demand for cheap labour intensified. The Chamber of Mines asked the government to provide a cheap labour supply. The South African government was willing to help the mine owners because it benefited from the gold mining industry, particularly through taxation.

Over time, the government introduced a number of measures to force more Africans to work in the mines. These included introducing taxes which only Africans had to pay, such as the **hut tax** and the **poll tax**. Most importantly, it passed the 1913 Land Act. This Act forced Africans to live in **reserves** and undermined the independence of African farmers by making it illegal for them to work as **sharecroppers**. This was clearly the beginning of territorial segregation, which will be explored in greater detail in the next chapter.

Why migrant labour?

The Chamber of Mines preferred to use migrant labour on the mines because they could pay the workers very low wages. They justified the low wages by claiming that the migrant worker's family earned an additional income in the reserves. Because migrant workers were supposedly only part-time workers, the mine owners did not have to provide them with any kind of social security.

Mine owners also preferred migrant labour because the workers could be controlled more easily. The men had signed employment contracts. If they broke their contracts by deserting, which many people did, they were arrested and got a criminal record. The migrants were also housed in closed compounds which were tightly controlled.

The conditions on the mines were very bad in the early decades. Workers often laboured fourteen hours a day. Deaths from major accidents, pneumonia, TB, **silicosis** and malnutrition were extremely high. On some mines, a hundred workers out of every thousand died each year.

Abe Bailey – a self-made man

There is no doubt that the Randlord, Abe Bailey, was a self-made man. His wealth enabled him to live a life of luxury and to enter into politics. But being rich and powerful did not necessarily make him a self-serving person. Abe Bailey became a noted **philanthropist**, making large donations to support the arts, sport and nature conservation. His son, Jim Bailey, founded the famous *Drum* magazine in 1951, followed by *Golden City Post*.

These publications provided a crucial outlet for black journalists and readers in the 1950s and 1960s. *Drum* played a particularly important role in documenting black culture and politics in the cities during a time of severe apartheid repression.

▲ *Abe Bailey, a Randlord and philanthropist who supported arts, sport and nature conservation.*

New words

independent peasant farmers – farmers who own their own plots of land (usually small) and live off the proceeds of the land

hut tax – all African communities had to pay a tax for each of their huts

poll tax – a tax of one pound (South Africa's currency at the time) for every adult male African

reserves – areas where it was legal for Africans to own or lease land

sharecroppers – farmers who lived and worked on white-owned farms. In exchange, they were expected to give half their crop to their landlords

silicosis – a disease caused by breathing in the dust that collects underground from drilling the rocks. This disease is also known as phthisis

philanthropist - a wealthy person who donates money to charity and to the promotion of good works in society

1. Many young South Africans today admire the notion of the 'self-made' man or woman. Entrepreneurship is seen as positive and is often encouraged, yet some of the information on the Randlords implies that the self-made person usually succeeds at the expense of the environment or other people. Do you think this is true?
   - Give an example of a self-made man or woman whose success was achieved at the expense of others. Give an example of a self-made man or woman whose success was achieved at the expense of the environment.
   - Give an example of a self-made man or woman whose success was achieved at no cost to the environment and other people.
2. Having considered these options, is the self-made man or woman a good thing or not? Debate this issue in class.

Mahudu Nkadimeng – a migrant worker

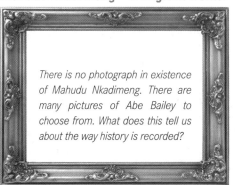

There is no photograph in existence of Mahudu Nkadimeng. There are many pictures of Abe Bailey to choose from. What does this tell us about the way history is recorded?

Self-made men often made their wealth through exploiting the labour of ordinary people. This was certainly the case in the mines. The Randlords could not have become so wealthy if they had not been able to exploit the labour of ordinary migrant workers. Mahudu Nkadimeng was one such ordinary migrant worker.

In the early 1900s, Mahudu Nkadimeng left Sekhukhuneland (today a district of Limpopo Province) and came to work on the gold mines as a migrant labourer. As a migrant worker, he rarely saw his family, and his son, John, grew up not knowing his father.

Men came to work on the mines as migrants for a whole variety of reasons. This extract from an interview conducted by social historian David Coplan, provides one explanation of why men came to Johannesburg:

> "I wanted to put on my trousers. I was ashamed of my loincloth, mostly because all the boys of my age were already regular miners that came back in their trousers, smoking cigarettes and speaking strange languages, relating exciting stories about their adventures."

▲ In Township Tonight *by D. Coplan, Ravan Press, Johannesburg, 1985.*

Mahudu Nkadimeng worked underground in the mines. Conditions underground were brutal. Both white and black underground workers faced the possibility of death through accidents in the form of rockfalls or from a number of respiratory diseases like TB, pneumonia and silicosis (phthisis). Mahudu Nkadimeng contracted silicosis from working underground. After a month-long, nightmarish journey on a donkey-cart, he returned home to Sekhukhuneland where he eventually died of the disease.

Although Mahudu Nkadimeng was just one of many thousands of migrant workers who lived and died in the mines of Johannesburg, this did not mean that the Nkadimeng family was lost to history. His son, John, grew up to be a noted trade union **activist**, who worked tirelessly for liberation in South Africa. In 1976 John Nkadimeng went into exile, only returning to South Africa in 1990. In the new South Africa, he served as our Ambassador to Cuba.

▲ *John Nkadimeng, the son of Mahudu Nkadimeng, as pictured on the ramp of the Apartheid Museum.*

What do these journeys tell us?

The journeys of both Abe Bailey and Mahudu Nkadimeng took unexpected turns. Their children did not necessarily follow the paths that history might have set for them. Jim Bailey did not use the wealth that he inherited from his father for his own purposes; rather, his magazines have contributed towards our understanding of urban black culture in the 1950s and 1960s. And John Nkadimeng, the son of a poor migrant worker, did not **sink into obscurity**. He played an important role in the liberation struggle, fighting for the dignity of workers through his trade union work.

New words

activist – a person who participates actively in a political movement in order to bring about change

sink into obscurity – disappear from the public eye and not be well-known by your society

Summative Assessment

GRADE 8: LO 1, AS 2
GRADE 9: LO 1, AS 3
GRADE 11: LO 1, AS 3

Look at all the sources that have been used in this chapter. Then, test your ability to understand and work with these sources by completing the table that follows.

The questions listed in the table are the kinds of questions that you should begin to ask of all sources.

Working with sources	Memory boxes	Photographs of Johannesburg	Diagram: What the mines needed	Quote from interview by historian, D. Coplan
1. Type of Source – written/ visual/oral/artefact/audio-visual				
2. Who wrote or produced the source?				
3. When was the source produced? At the time, or long after the event?				
4. What is the point of view of the person who wrote or produced the source? (*)				
5. Do you trust this source? Give reasons for your answer. (*)				

CHAPTER 2

SEGREGATION IN ACTION

GRADE 8
Content: Industrialization in South Africa: changing work and lives in South Africa on the mines, the land and in the cities.

GRADE 11
Content: How unique was apartheid - how was segregation a foundation for apartheid?

KEEPING PEOPLE APART

The Apartheid Museum displays this wall-sized photograph of hundreds of miners of all races, sitting together. It is a relaxed photo and there is a sense of ease and naturalness. But the **municipal authorities** and the mining bosses, or Randlords, did not approve of this racial mixing.

They wanted blacks and whites to be kept apart in all areas of possible contact – where they lived, at work, in running the government and in public places. They created laws and forced separation on the people. This was the beginning of segregation.

Segregation and early Johannesburg

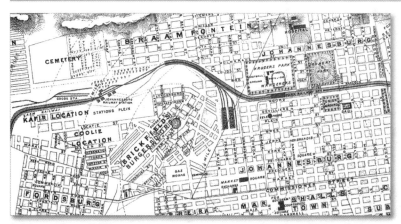

▲ Johannesburg, 1897.

A few steps away from the photograph of the miners, hangs one of the earliest maps of Johannesburg, published in 1897. It shows that, from the earliest days, the municipal authorities planned to keep the different racial groups apart. There are different areas clearly marked out for African, coloured, Indian and white residents.

1. What do the names of certain areas tell us about the way that municipal authorities viewed blacks?
2. From an analysis of the map and the accompanying text, where do you think racial mixing was the greatest? Explain your answer.
3. The gold reef in Johannesburg ran from east to west. Bearing this in mind, explain why the railway line was built in the position it was. (∗)
4. What does the phrase 'from the wrong side of the tracks' mean? (∗)
5. Do you think north or south was 'the wrong side of the tracks' on this map? Explain your answer. (∗)

GRADE 8: LO 1, AS 2
GRADE 9: LO 1, AS 3
GRADE 11: LO 1, AS 3 and 4

To begin with, however, segregation was not strictly applied and racial mixing amongst the poor was a common feature of early Johannesburg. For example, Burgersdorp was supposed to be an all-white suburb, and was inhabited largely by working class Afrikaners. Yet very soon, blacks also began to live in the area.

As more and more people flocked to the Rand in search of work, slums developed in the poorer areas. Because the **slums** were underserviced and overcrowded, diseases often broke out in these areas. In 1904, there was an outbreak of **bubonic plague** in the '**Coolie**' Location and the Brickfields. Instead of dealing with the causes of disease, the municipal authorities used this as an excuse to burn down the 'Coolie' Location.

The Africans who lived in the 'Coolie' Location were removed to Klipspruit. This was twenty kilometres outside of town and was to become the first suburb of Soweto many years later.

New words

municipal authorities – the local town or city council responsible for the administration of the town or city, elected by white ratepayers

slums – areas of a town or a city where very poor people live in extremely overcrowded and neglected conditions

bubonic plague – a disease that swept through Europe in the fourteenth century and took the lives of millions of people. It eventually spread across the world through trade and was carried by rats in slums like the 'Coolie' Location.

'Coolie' – an offensive word for Indian

▲ *The Apartheid Museum displays this photograph, which shows the burning down of the 'Coolie' Location.*

GRADE 8

Content: Industrialization in South Africa: changing work and lives in South Africa on the mines, the land and in the cities.

GRADE 11

Content: How was segregation a foundation for apartheid?

SEGREGATION AS POLICY

In 1910 South Africa was united for the first time into a single state known as the Union of South Africa. Racial segregation became official policy throughout the Union and laid the foundation for apartheid.

▲ *The two key politicians at the time, General Jan Smuts and General J.B.M. Hertzog, were strongly in favour of segregating South African society. They introduced segregation into the city, the workplace and politics.*

Sol Plaatje, an African writer and member of the South African Native National Congress, travelled all over the country finding out about the effects of the 1913 Land Act. Here, he describes the horrors facing an African family who had been evicted from a white-owned farm. The family was on the road, looking for somewhere to settle, when one of their children died.

The deceased child had to be buried, but where, when and how? Even criminals dropping straight from the gallows have an undisputed claim to six feet of ground on which to rest their criminal remains, but under the cruel operation of the Land Act little children, whose only crime is that God did not make them white, are sometimes denied that right in their ancestral home.

Adapted from Native Life in South Africa, *by Sol T. Plaatje*

TERRITORIAL SEGREGATION: Key legislation

Of South Africa's total population of 5 972 577 in 1911, 21% were white, 8.8% were coloured, 2.5% were Asian and 67.7% were African.

The Land Act (1913):

One of the first formal acts of segregation in the Union of South Africa, this Act forced Africans to live in **reserves**, which made up only 8.7 % of the country's land. We call this **territorial segregation**. The 1913 Land Act undermined the independence of African farmers by making it illegal for them to work as share-croppers or to be rent-paying tenants. Africans living on white farms were now forced to work for wages, or to give 90 days' free labour in exchange for the use of a piece of land for a year.

The Natives' Trust and Land Act (1936):

This Act made more land available in the African reserves, increasing them to 13% of the land. It also created a Native Trust to control the reserves. The authorities hoped more Africans would be able to live and work in the reserves and would not need to move to the urban areas to look for work.

Segregating the city

By 1923, about 126 000 Africans were living on the **Rand**, including 13 000 women and 25 000 children. The municipal authorities were worried about the number of Africans, and particularly women, who were moving into towns. Some white people feared that they would be 'swamped' by so many Africans moving to the towns.

Residential segregation

The prime minister of South Africa at the time was Jan Smuts. He strongly supported the idea of **residential segregation** between blacks and whites. Johannesburg was the largest urban centre in the country and the most racially-mixed.

In 1922 the Stallard Commission was appointed by the Transvaal Local Government to investigate the presence of Africans in towns. As a result of the recommendations of the Stallard Commission, the Native (Urban Areas) Act was passed by the Smuts government in 1923.

This Act called for the clearance of the slums and gave municipal authorities powers to establish separate **locations** for Africans throughout the country, usually at the edges of towns.

Natives – men, women and children – should only be allowed in urban areas when their presence is demanded by the wants of the white population.

▲ *Stallard investigated the presence of Africans in towns in 1922.*

▲ *New locations, such as Nancefield, were established to the south west of Johannesburg beyond the municipal boundaries.*

Influx control

An important aspect of urban segregation was **influx control**. The central government tried to limit the flow of Africans into towns by controlling who was allowed in the urban areas. They did this through the use of passes. Every African man had to carry a pass which gave him permission to be in an urban area. Only people who could find work were given a pass. As a result, people accepted whatever jobs they could find, often for very low wages. If an African male was unable to find work in the urban areas, he was forced to return to the rural areas.

Police conducted regular pass raids. If a person's pass was not in order, or if they did not have a pass in their possession, they were arrested, kicked out of the urban areas and sent back to the reserves.

These pass raids happened so often, that most Africans had, at one time or another, been arrested for a pass law offence. This had the effect of turning the majority of the African population into criminals.

New words

reserves – rural areas where it was legal for Africans to own or lease land.

territorial segregation – the division of South Africa's rural areas into separate portions. The majority of the land was set aside for whites, while Africans were only allowed to live in the reserves.

Rand – the area around Johannesburg

residential segregation – the creation of separate living areas in the towns and cities to ensure that people of different races lived apart

locations – residential areas or townships set aside for Africans. They were usually established just outside so-called white areas.

influx control – the policy of restricting the numbers of African people allowed to live and work in the towns and cities, through the use of passes

RESIDENTIAL SEGREGATION: Key segregationist legislation

The Urban Areas Native Pass Act (1909):
This Act was intended to control the movement of Africans into towns. It provided work seekers with a permit, which allowed them six days to find work. If they did not find work, they had to return to the rural areas.

The Natives (Urban Areas) Act (1923):
This Act established segregated locations where Africans had to live.

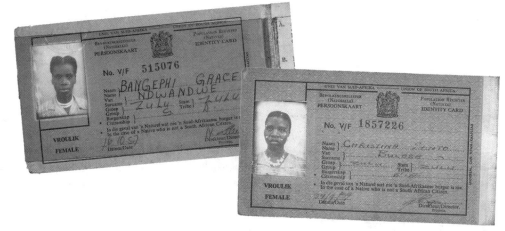

▲ *The Apartheid Museum has on display a number of original passes and ID documents.*

Below are two sources on the pass laws. The first is a poem and the second is an extract from an autobiography.

Kwela-Ride
A poem by Mafika Gwala

Dompas*!*
I looked back
Dompas!
I went through my pockets
Not there.

They bit into my flesh
(handcuffs).

Came the **kwela-kwela**
We crawled in.
The young men sang.
In that dark moment

It all became familiar.

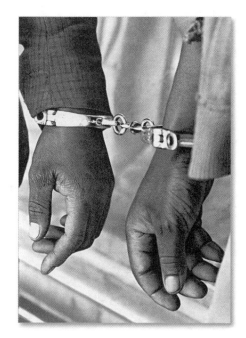

Blame Me on History
An extract from Bloke Modisane's autobiography

This is the essence of the Pass Law.
I cannot sell my labour to the highest bidder.
I cannot live in the residential area of my choice; I am committed by the colour of my skin to live in segregated ghettos or locations or slums.
Freedom of movement is restricted by the **Reference Book.**
The right to live in peace in my house is subject to the pleasure of any superintendent or Native Commissioner who is empowered to **endorse me out** *of the municipal district if, in his opinion, my presence is a danger to public peace and good order.*
This is the law.

Read the two sources on the pass laws again, and then answer the following questions:
1. Why do you think the speaker is being arrested in the poem *Kwela-Ride*?
2. Do you think this event has happened to him more than once? Give a reason.
3. Bloke Modisane says that his "freedom of movement is restricted by the Reference Book". What do you think he means by this? Give some examples from the extract which show how his freedom of movement was restricted.
4. How do both pieces of writing show that the pass laws limited the freedom of movement of Africans? (∗)
5. What is the attitude of both writers to the pass laws? Give an example from each piece of writing to explain your answer. (∗)

GRADE 8: LO 3, AS 1 and 4
GRADE 9: LO 1, AS 3; LO 3, AS 3
GRADE 11: LO 1, AS 3; LO 3, AS 3

Activity 3: Developing empathy in history

Imagine that you are an African man living in Johannesburg in 1924. You have just been arrested because you did not have a permit in your pass allowing you to be in an urban area. Write a letter to the *Sunday Times* in which you explain how the pass laws have affected your life. Your letter must be based on real evidence. You must gain your information from the following sources:
• information that you have gathered from the two pieces of writing on the pass laws on page 26.
• interviewing a person who had to carry a pass in Apartheid South Africa. Ask him/her to describe what it felt like to carry a pass and to be arrested for a pass offence. (Remember that, after 1956, African women also had to carry passes.)

GRADE 8: LO 1, AS 5; LO 3, AS 4
GRADE 9: LO 1, AS 5; LO 3, AS 3
GRADE 11: LO 1, AS 3; LO 3, AS 2 and 4

SEGREGATING THE WORKPLACE

GRADE 8
Content: Industrialization in South Africa: changing work and lives in South Africa on the mines, the land and in the cities.

GRADE 11
Content: How was segregation a foundation for apartheid?

In 1922, white workers on the mines went on a general strike. They were protesting against the proposal by the Chamber of Mines to replace white workers with black workers. The slogan of some white miners was 'Workers of the World Unite and Fight for a White S.A.' as can be seen in this photograph in the Apartheid Museum.

The strike was brutally suppressed by the Smuts government. This was one reason why Smuts lost the 1924 general election, after which General Hertzog became prime minister of the Union of South Africa.

Hertzog formed the Pact Government – a political alliance between his Afrikaner-based National Party and the Labour Party led by Colonel F.H.P. Creswell. Although these two parties had some different beliefs, they both disliked Smuts. They believed that Smuts and his South African Party (SAP) was not doing enough to protect white workers from losing their jobs to African workers.

▲ *Poor whites on the Rand in the 1930s.*

SEGREGATING
THE WORKPLACE:
Key legislation

The Mines and Works Act (1911):
This Act reserved certain skilled work on the mines for whites.

The Industrial Conciliation Act (1924):
This Act set up industrial councils, where trade unions could negotiate with employers. It excluded Africans from membership of trade unions, and as a result, from industrial councils.

The Wages Act (1925):
This Act set compulsory minimum wages for white workers in unskilled jobs.

The Mines and Works Amendment Act (1926):
This was also known as the Colour Bar Act. It excluded Africans and Indians from skilled work. Certificates of competency for trades in the mines could be issued only to whites and to coloureds in certain occupations.

Hertzog was particularly concerned about protecting the Afrikaners, who were his main supporters. There had been an influx of **poor whites** (mainly Afrikaners) onto the Witwatersrand and it was important for Hertzog to provide them with work. The Pact Government also wanted to reduce South Africa's dependence on the mining industry. Hertzog believed that the development of **secondary industry** would solve both problems. It would provide work in factories for poor whites and reduce South Africa's economic dependence on mining.

The 'civilized labour' policy

Poor whites who moved to the towns and cities had little education and few skills. The only work that they were able to do was unskilled work, but Africans were usually used for unskilled work as their labour was cheaper. In order to ensure that white workers were protected from black competition, the 'civilized labour policy' was introduced from 1924 onwards.

This policy meant that whites would be paid a much higher wage – 'a civilized wage' – for doing the same work as Africans. Unskilled white workers were also favoured over unskilled Africans, particularly in the civil service and railways.

The 'civilized labour' policy was expensive, because employers had to pay white workers more than they would have had to pay African workers. It is clear that the government wanted segregation in the workplace even though it was much more expensive.

A biased source is one that supports only one side or shows only one point of view. It also shows the **prejudices** of the writer. Although biased sources may only show one side of events, they can be useful because they show us how different people thought and felt about things in the past.

How to identify bias in a source:
— The writer may use **emotive** words which arouse strong feelings in the readers. Look for certain words in the text which arouse strong emotions in you.
— Knowledge of the writer's background and world view/beliefs can help to reveal bias. Sometimes the person may support a particular cause or a group. Ask who wrote the source and what the person believed.
— Sometimes the source has been written with a specific purpose in mind. Ask why the person wrote or created the source.

New words

poor whites – usually Afrikaners, who had been forced off the land, either through drought or poor farming methods, and had moved to the towns and cities

secondary industry – industry which processes raw materials and makes them into something manufactured, usually in a factory

prejudices – strong beliefs or opinions either firmly in favour of or against a person or a thing

emotive - arousing strong feelings and emotions

Activity 4: **Analysing a variety of sources on segregation in the workplace**

▲ This cartoon was used in the election campaign in 1924. 'Spoorwee' means railways.

1. Who does the person entering the railways in this cartoon represent?
2. Who does the person being kicked out of the railways represent?
3. What does the cartoon suggest about the nature of employment on the railways?
4. How does the cartoon help us to understand white workers' fears about African labour? (∗)
5. Why did white workers have such fears? (∗)
6. In what way is this cartoon critical of Smuts and his South African Party (SAP)? (∗)
7. How did the 'civilized labour' policy hope to reassure white workers that there was no real basis for their fears? (∗)

GRADE 8: LO 1, AS 2; LO 3, AS 2
GRADE 11: LO 1, AS 4; LO 2, AS 1; LO 3, AS 2

'Civilized labour' is work done by people whose standard of living conforms to the decent standard of white living, while 'uncivilized labour' is work done by persons whose goals or aim is restricted to basic necessities of underdeveloped and 'savage' people.

▲ Extract from Hertzog's circular to government departments, 31 October 1924.

1. This source is a government circular. What does this tell you about the attitude and beliefs of the Pact Government?
2. In what way is this source a biased source? (*)
   a. Has the writer used any words that arouse strong emotion in you? Which words do this and what feelings do they arouse?
   b. Who do you think wrote this kind of source? What do you think his attitude and beliefs were?
   c. What was the purpose of this source? What reasons would the writer have had for creating this source?
3. Would you expect to find such language in a government circular today? What does this tell you about the attitude and beliefs of the current government? (*)

SEGREGATING POLITICAL RIGHTS

Hertzog believed that political segregation was essential for the survival of whites as the dominant group in society. When the Union of South Africa was created in 1910, black people were formally denied the right to vote, with one exception. Some African and coloured men living in the Cape were allowed to vote if they had a certain level of education and owned some property. This was known as a **qualified franchise**.

In 1926 Hertzog introduced the 'Hertzog Native Bills' into parliament. These aimed to remove Cape Africans from the Cape **voters' roll**. At the same time, he supported giving coloureds the vote in all provinces, not just the Cape. It appears that Hertzog hoped to integrate coloureds into white society in order to strengthen his own political support.

The Hertzog Native Representation Bill was criticized, both inside and outside parliament and it was only ten years later, in 1936, that it eventually became law. Why did it take such a long time to become law? One of the reasons is that Smuts had opposed the bill in 1926 because he needed the Cape African vote to hold onto vital seats for his South Africa Party in parliament. As a result, Hertzog was unable to get enough support in parliament for it to be passed, but by 1936, Smuts and Hertzog had joined together in a new political party – the United Party. Hertzog now had enough support in parliament for the bill to be passed.

Throughout this period, the ANC opposed the Hertzog 'Native' Bills. They argued that Africans formed the majority of the population and should not be denied a say in government.

RESISTANCE TO SEGREGATION

The extension of segregation between 1910 and 1937, which is dealt with in the Segregation Hall of the Apartheid Museum, led to resistance from African, coloured and Indian communities across the country.

The ANC

The South African National Native Congress, as the ANC was first called, was established in 1912, largely as a response to the proposed Land Bill (which became the 1913 Land Act). In its early years, the ANC was a fairly small and **moderate** organization. It drew its membership largely from the educated African **elite**.

The leadership of the ANC believed that if they responded reasonably to injustices, white politicians would take them seriously. They therefore used petitions, **delegations** and resolutions as a form of protest. Unfortunately, white politicians tended to dismiss these measures completely.

SEGREGATING POLITICAL RIGHTS:
Key legislation

The Native Representation Act (1936):
This Act removed Cape Africans from the common voters' roll and provided Africans with their own separate institution – the Native Representative Council (NRC). Through the NRC, Africans could make recommendations to parliament about issues that affected them.

The Native Trust and Land Act (1936):
This Act increased the land which Africans could own from 8.7% to 13% of all land in South Africa. But it placed more controls over labour tenancy on farms.

The Native Laws Amendment Act (1937):
This Act strengthened influx control. Local authorities could now refuse Africans entry to towns and force them into the reserves if they did not have jobs.

◀ A delegation of the SANNC went to London to protest against the Land Act. It consisted of (l to r) Thomas Mapikela, Rev Walter Rubusana, Rev John Dube, Saul Msane and Sol Plaatje.

Indian passive resistance

The Indian community was inspired by the leadership of Mohandas Gandhi, a lawyer who had come from India to work with the Indian community in Natal in 1893. He used the principle of *satyagraha* as the basis of a non-violent protest strategy in which Indians aimed to be arrested by gathering in large numbers to protest against unjust laws.

In 1913 Indian workers went on strike to protest against the **discriminatory laws** against Indians, especially the £3 (three pounds) annual tax they were forced to pay and their poor working conditions. Thousands of people, including Gandhi, were jailed.

Gandhi believed that if the prisons were overflowing, the government would be forced to negotiate with the Indian community. Eventually, the government did enter into negotiations with Gandhi and the new laws were **repealed.**

▲ Gandhi, third from the left, leading a protest march in 1913.

The APO

The African People's Organization (APO) was founded in Cape Town in 1902. Dr Abdullah Abdurahman became the leader in 1905 and led it for 35 years. The APO fought for the rights of coloured people. Its membership consisted largely of the coloured elite, and it also used petitions and delegations as a form of protest. These tended to be ignored by white politicians. After 1910, the APO tried to link up with African organizations to oppose white domination.

The AAC

The All-African Convention (AAC) was formed in 1935 with the specific intention of opposing Hertzog's 'Native' Bills. It appealed to the British government for help and sent a deputation to meet with Hertzog, but all this had no effect.

Despite formal AAC protest meetings throughout the country, the Native Representation Act was passed in 1936. Having lost that battle, the AAC and the ANC had to decide how to respond to the Native Representative Council (NRC), which was set up by the government as an African advisory body. They could boycott the NRC or participate in it. They eventually agreed to participate, but the NRC had no real power. The AAC and ANC later called it a 'toy telephone', because nobody listened to them when they used it.

The ICU: A taste of freedom

A more effective African protest in the 1920s came from the Industrial and Commercial Workers Union, known as the ICU. What was remarkable about the ICU was both its rapid rise – by 1928, it had a membership of over 100 000 - and its rapid fall. By 1930, the ICU had lost its strength and had faded into insignificance.

Although the ICU began as a trade union of African dockworkers in Cape Town in 1918, it gradually transformed itself into a mass movement in the late 1920s. The reason for the brief success of the ICU in this period was its ability to respond to important issues on the ground which affected Africans directly. In particular, the ICU shifted its attention to the countryside, especially in Natal and the Orange Free State, where African farm workers were being evicted or facing wage cuts. The ICU organized **non-co-operation**, acts of violence on a number of farms and legal challenges in the courts.

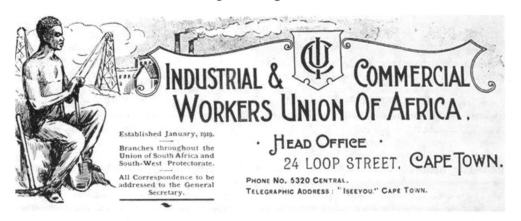

Activity 5: Developing arguments

Copy and complete the following table to show the effectiveness of various forms of resistance to segregation.

	Methods used	Effectiveness: Mark out of 10	Evidence to support your mark
ANC			
Indian resistance			
APO			
AAC			
ICU			

▲ *Adapted from C. Culpin,* South Africa since 1948, *John Murray, 2000.*

SKILLS **Developing essay writing skills: one main idea per paragraph**

When writing a history essay, it is important to structure your ideas in a clear and organized way. A good rule to remember is that you should only have one main or controlling idea in each paragraph.

A good paragraph will start with a clear sentence introducing the main idea of the paragraph. This should be followed by evidence or examples which illustrate the point made in this first sentence. The paragraph should end with a concluding sentence which links the point you have made to the overall topic or argument you are making.

An example

Main sentence:

In its early years, the ANC did not resist segregation very effectively because it lacked the power to challenge the government.

Evidence or example to support main sentence:

For example, the ANC protested against the Land Act by sending delegations to meet the government. These delegations achieved little success.

Concluding sentence:

Because the ANC had no real power at this time, the government largely ignored their protests.

Activity 6: **Writing paragraphs with only one main idea (∗)**

Here is a possible essay topic:

To what extent was early resistance to segregation effective?

- Use the guidelines in the skills box for writing a paragraph.
- Use the information from the table that you filled out in Activity 5 to write a few paragraphs which address this question.
- Each paragraph should deal with one of the organizations in the table.
- Each paragraph should answer the essay question by discussing one specific organization.

GRADE 11: LO 3, AS 2
GRADE 12: LO 3, AS 2

THE GREAT DEPRESSION

GRADE 8
Content: Industrialization in South Africa: changing work and lives in South Africa on the mines, the land and in the cities.

GRADE 11
Content: How was segregation a foundation for apartheid?

In 1929, the Wall Street Stock Exchange in New York collapsed and this plunged the world into an economic depression. The period of history from 1929 to the mid-1930s is known as the Great Depression. All countries, including South Africa, faced economic and social crisis.

▲ *The world tightens its belt.*

People could no longer afford to buy anything, so mines and factories closed down. Thousands of people lost their jobs. African workers were usually the first to lose their jobs. People living in the countryside were particularly badly hit. Not only could farmers no longer sell their products, but a major drought destroyed their crops.

Africans were already experiencing hardship in the reserves. The Depression forced thousands to move to the cities in search of work. In particular, African women began to enter the cities in large numbers, hoping to find work as domestic servants, washerwomen or beer brewers.

Many Afrikaners who had been living as **bywoners** on the land, flocked to the cities, joining the ranks of the poor whites.

As the poor moved into the cities, racial divisions blurred and blacks and whites lived together in slum areas. This worried the government and made them intensify their segregationist policies. The government also took many steps to improve conditions for poor whites. Although poor Africans experienced poverty just as intensely as poor whites, the government viewed Africans as a problem that they had to get rid of. As a result, they applied the pass laws much more strictly to try to prevent Africans from moving to the cities.

▲ *A soup kitchen for poor whites in the 1930s.*

Zack Zampetakis remembers what it was like growing up as a young Greek boy during the Depression.

"As far as I can remember we were the only whites living with blacks – with coloureds and blacks. We were sharing our rooms. In the front bedroom was a coloured woman living there. The lounge was our bedroom, and the dining room was occupied by an African man and his wife. We were all well integrated, we all had very few problems with each other. There was a sense of community, a sense of belonging too.

It was the time of the Depression ... Our meals consisted of beans, string beans. This was our staple food – we had that and nothing else, just the bread. The Transvaal Helping Hand Society used to hand us food parcels, which my mother used to sell in order to clothe me. At school, they put me apart in class because I was covered in sores, and because the other mothers protested that their kids were sitting next to this child who had vuilsiekte, which means filthy disease."

▲ *Adapted from* Working Life *by L. Callinicos, Ravan Press, 1987, pp. 234-236.*

▲ *The government gave African children no support during the Great Depression.*

Es'kia Mphahlele remembers what it was like to be a young African boy who lived during the Depression.

*"I did most of the domestic work, because my sister and brother were still too small. I woke up at 4.30 in the morning to make a fire in a **brazier** made out of an old lavatory bucket. I washed and made breakfast for the family. Back from school I had to clean the house as Aunt Dora and grandmother did the white people's washing all day.*

*Because we were so many in the family, there was only one bedstead. The wooden floor of the room we slept in had two large holes. There was always a sharp **draught** coming up from underneath the floor. Coupled with this our heads were a playground for mice which also **created havoc** with our food and clothing.*

▲ *Adapted from E. Mphahlele,* Down Second Avenue, *pp. 23-24.*

New words

brazier – pan or stand for holding burning coals

draught – a current of cold air in a confined space

created havoc – caused chaos and destruction

Activity 7: Using oral history to gain understanding of the Depression

1. What does the young Greek boy's experience tell us about racial mixing amongst the poor?
2. According to the young Greek boy, what kind of aid did poor whites receive?
3. Why do you think Es'kia Mphahlele did not receive such aid?
4. Why did Es'kia Mphahlele have to do so much housework?
5. Compare the experiences of these two children during the Great Depression. What is similar and what is different about their experiences?

GRADE 8: LO 3, AS 7
GRADE 11: LO 2, AS 3

Activity 8: Focusing on memory and oral history (*)

1. How do these memories help you to understand what life was like for children during the Depression?
2. How do the experiences of these children growing up in the Depression compare with your own experiences of growing up?
3. Keeping in mind that these are the memories of adults who are remembering events that took place a long time ago, do you think that these are reliable sources? How would you test their reliability?

GRADE 11: LO 1, AS 4; LO 2, AS 3

Activity 9: Finding out about your own history

1. Conduct an interview with an older person about a difficult time that they experienced and overcame a long time ago. This person may be a member of your family or a member of your community.
2. When you have finished the interview, try to find out some more information about this event from other sources, e.g. written sources or photographs. You should try to see how accurate the person's memory of the event is.

GRADE 8: LO 3, AS 7
GRADE 9: LO 3, AS 4
GRADE 11: LO 2, AS 3; LO 4, AS 3

CHAPTER 3

THE IMPLEMENTATION OF APARTHEID

GRADE 11
Content: How was segregation
a foundation for apartheid?

THE GROWTH OF AFRIKANER NATIONALISM

In the 1930s Afrikaner nationalism was growing stronger. It stressed the **uniqueness** of Afrikaners as God's chosen people and became linked with ideas of racial superiority. These ideas would develop into the policy of apartheid.

There were a number of regroupings in white politics in the 1930s. In 1934, Prime Minister J.B.M. Hertzog was losing support because of the economic crisis resulting from a combination of the Great Depression and a **devastating** drought. In order to stay in power, he joined with Smuts to form the United Party. Dr D.F. Malan, a minister in Hertzog's government, saw this alliance as a betrayal of the Afrikaner and walked out. Together with his followers, he formed a new party, the Purified National Party.

Malan and his followers believed that the Afrikaner was in danger of being politically **undermined** by the English and economically threatened by Indians and Jews, as well as by Africans who were competing with poor white Afrikaners for unskilled work in the cities. They also believed that South Africa should not be a **monarchy**; but a **republic**.

Afrikaners face a new trek – to the city. There black and white compete in the same labour market. The task is to make South Africa a white man's land.

◀ *Dr D.F. Malan led the movement to promote Afrikaner Nationalism. He stressed the racial superiority of Afrikaners over blacks.*

The Great Trek Centenary

In 1918, a group of Afrikaners formed a secret organization called the Broederbond to promote Afrikaner Nationalism. They believed that Afrikaners needed to develop a sense of pride in their identity and culture in order to withstand the threat from both the English and Africans.

In 1938, the Broederbond organized the Great Trek **Centenary** celebrations to promote Afrikaner Nationalism. To Afrikaner Nationalists, the Great Trek represented their triumph over both the British and the Africans.

The Apartheid Museum provides a unique opportunity to experience the creation of Afrikaner Nationalism by watching a film called Bou van 'n Nasie (They Built a Nation). This is a **propaganda** film made in 1938 as part of the build up to the Centenary celebrations. In this film, Afrikaner history is presented as a powerful and successful struggle against **hostile** forces.

New words

uniqueness – having no equal, being the only one of their kind

devastating – causing great destruction and, in this case, financial ruin

undermined – made gradually weaker or less effective

monarchy – a form of government where a monarch (in South Africa's case, the King of England) is the head of state

republic – a form of government where South Africa would rule itself and have no constitutional ties to Britain

centenary – celebration of the hundredth anniversary

propaganda – deliberately using information in order to influence the way that people think and behave

hostile – unfriendly and aggressive

◀ *One hundred thousand Afrikaners, many dressed in Voortrekker clothing, gathered at the site of the future Voortrekker Monument to greet the teams of trekkers and ox-wagons who had travelled from Cape Town to Pretoria. There, the new anthem* Die Stem van Suid Afrika *was sung enthusiastically.*

Activity 1: The symbols of Afrikaner Nationalism

1. The use of **symbols** was important in the construction of Afrikaner Nationalism. List all the symbols in the above photograph of the Great Trek Centenary.
2. Explain what each symbol stood for.
3. How do you think that these symbols helped to build a feeling of Afrikaner identity? (∗)
4. What symbols do other nationalist movements around the world use? (∗)
5. Do you think that nationalist symbols are a good or a bad thing? Discuss this issue in class. (∗)

GRADE 9: LO 3, AS 4
GRADE 11: LO 4, AS 1

THE FORTIES – A DECADE OF UPHEAVAL

GRADE 9
Content: Apartheid in South Africa: the impact of World War Two

GRADE 11
Content: How was segregation a foundation for apartheid?

World War Two (1939-1945) led to a period of huge change and **upheaval**. African working people, confronted with rising prices, low wages and shortages of food and housing, became increasingly **radicalized**. Ordinary people began organizing around these problems and the 1940s saw a number of community protests, such as squatter movements and bus boycotts.

African urbanization

The number of Africans, especially women, coming to the cities increased enormously. By now, many Africans living in cities were no longer migrants, but settled and permanent city dwellers. By 1946, there were more blacks than whites living in cities for the first time.

The increased numbers of Africans coming to the city put pressure on housing and local municipal authorities could not cope. By 1940 there were four municipal housing schemes for Africans in Johannesburg: Western Native Township, Eastern Native Township, Orlando and Pimville. However, there was massive overcrowding in these areas and the accommodation was hopelessly inadequate.

People also lived in the **freehold** townships of Alexandra in the north-east of Johannesburg, and Sophiatown, Martindale and Newclare in the west. By the 1940s, they too were experiencing severe overcrowding problems.

What was happening in white politics?

When World War Two began, the United Party, led by Hertzog, was in power. Hertzog did not want South Africa to go to war against Germany. The issue was debated in parliament and 80 MPs voted in favour of going to war and 67 voted against it. Hertzog therefore resigned and Smuts took over as prime minister and leader of the United Party.

An extreme **right-wing** Afrikaner organization which supported Hitler and was called the *Ossewa Brandwag*, engaged in acts of sabotage during World War Two.

Who was James Mpanza?

urbanization – when large numbers of people move from the countryside to the towns and cities

freehold – areas where blacks were allowed to own property. They were also relatively free from strict municipal control

controversial – in this case, controversial means that there were many disagreements about him

devastating – destructive

verify – to establish the truth or correctness of something

▲ Mpanza, in the middle, drew support from the women of Orlando because he offered them and their families security in a time of social upheaval.

James Mpanza was a popular leader who organized a squatter movement of the homeless in Orlando. Through his actions, the municipal authorities were eventually forced to provide housing for the squatters. However, James Mpanza was an extremely **controversial** man. In the Apartheid Museum you can see an excellent video about Mpanza that highlights the controversy surrounding him. Here are two extracts from the video in which William Carr and Walter Sisulu express different views about Mpanza.

Mpanza was a brilliant chap. He was a thinker. Very stylish too in his actions. He could be **devastating** when dealing with the opposition. In jail he became a preacher, and created a good impression. He was finally released from prison. You see all this sea of houses ... it is a result of Mpanza.

▲ Walter Sisulu, who went on to become the secretary-general of the ANC, was a resident of Soweto at the time of Mpanza's squatter movement.

Mpanza was a Zulu who had been arrested, tried for murder and sentenced to death. And it would have saved a good deal of trouble for everyone if the sentence had been carried out... He was a criminal, a thug. He was a man of very bad character. He stole money. He was always drunk. He was a pest!

▲ William Carr, the Johannesburg City Council's Manager of Non-European Affairs, took a hard line on Mpanza.

Skills development: differentiating between facts and opinions

A fact is something which is known to have taken place, and can be proved.
An opinion is usually based on someone's belief, and need not necessarily be based on fact.

All historians are concerned with the reliability of a source. Sources which contain facts that can be proved are usually more reliable than sources which are based mostly on opinion. However, a source that contains more opinion than fact can be a useful source because it tells us what people felt and believed at certain times in history.

When you find sources that contain more opinions than facts, it is often difficult to work out what really happened or what the person was really like. When this happens, it is important to consult other sources. In this way, you can **verify** the facts and opinions.

Activity 2: Dealing with contradictory sources

Step 1: Identifying facts and opinions

Using the views about Mpanza expressed by William Carr and Walter Sisulu, copy and complete the following table:

	Facts	Opinions
William Carr		
Walter Sisulu		

GRADE 9: LO 1, AS 2; LO 3, AS 1
GRADE 11: LO 1, AS 4

Step 2: Testing contradictory sources for reliability

1. Whose statement contains more facts about Mpanza – Carr's or Sisulu's?
2. Consider each of the statements that you have entered in the facts column for both Carr and Sisulu. For which of these statements could you find evidence against which you can check whether or not it is true? What kinds of evidence could you use? (*)
3. Which source do you think is more reliable? Walter Sisulu or William Carr? Or are neither reliable? Give a reason for your answer. (*)
4. Despite the fact that these sources are contradictory, explain in what ways they may be useful to a person studying this period in history. (*)

Activity 3: Research project (*)

GRADE 11: LO 3, AS 4

James Mpanza – local hero or villain?

If you want to find out more about James Mpanza, you will have to do extra research. Read up about James Mpanza at your local or school library or in your history textbooks. Try to gather as many facts about James Mpanza as possible. If you live in Soweto, you could also ask older members of your community if they have any memories of Mpanza.

Report your findings to the class. What have you all found out? What is your opinion of James Mpanza now?

GRADE 9:
Content: Apartheid in
South Africa: the impact of
World War Two

GRADE 11
Content: How was segregation
a foundation for apartheid?

WHY DID THE NATIONALISTS WIN THE 1948 ELECTION?

After the War

After World War Two South Africa experienced serious economic problems. Both blacks and whites faced rising costs and housing shortages. The great influx of Africans to the cities heightened the racial tensions that already existed in South Africa. The growth of shanty towns and squatter movements aroused white fears of being **swamped** by growing numbers of Africans moving into the cities.

During the War, many Africans had become factory workers and black trade unions grew larger. Many whites feared the economic and political challenges presented by the black trade unions and the threat they posed to white privileges.

New words

swamped – overwhelmed by

constituencies – South Africa was divided into about 150 constituencies. Each constituency was represented by one MP in parliament

▲ *White fears strengthened when 70 000 African mineworkers went on strike in 1946 demanding wage increases and family housing.*

In late 1946, Prime Minister Jan Smuts appointed the Fagan Commission to investigate the best way to deal with the problem of African urbanization. At the same time, the National Party, led by Dr D.F. Malan, appointed its own commission, the Sauer Commission.

Recommendations of the Fagan Report, February 1948

- Total segregation would never work.
- Industry and commerce needed a permanent and settled black urban population.
- It was impossible to return all the existing townspeople to the reserves, which were already overcrowded.
- Migrant labour should be discouraged.
- African families should be encouraged to settle in locations under strict controls.

Recommendations of the Sauer Report, 1948

Apartheid or the separate development of the races was the only way forward.
- The reserves were where Africans belonged.
- The flood of Africans into the cities was a dangerous development.
- Urban Africans must continue to be treated as visitors without political rights.
- Their numbers must be strictly controlled.
- The migrant labour system must continue.
- Black locations must be kept clearly separate from white towns.

Many whites felt that, as prime minister, Jan Smuts was not doing enough to address their fears. In 1948, the National Party won the general election. Its election slogan had been 'Apartheid'. Once the Nationalists were in power, they gradually began to implement the recommendations of the Sauer Report.

Activity 4: Analysing sources

1. Which political party accepted the findings of the Fagan Report?
2. Which political party accepted the findings of the Sauer Report?
3. What are the major differences between the Fagan and Sauer Reports?
4. Which report do you think the majority of white South Africans would have preferred? Give reasons for your answer. (∗)
5. What effect do you think these reports would have had on the 1948 election? (∗)
6. How different might the course of South African history have been if Fagan's recommendations, rather than Sauer's, had been implemented? (∗)

GRADE 9: LO 1, AS 3
GRADE 11: LO 1, AS 3

SKILLS **Developing essay writing skills: analysing the essay question**

When writing history essays, it is extremely important always to analyse the essay question before starting to write.
- Every history essay is a question not a topic. A topic includes all information on a subject. A question asks you to consider a certain issue or aspect of a topic.
- Every history essay asks you to develop an argument in relation to a particular problem that is posed. This usually involves stating an opinion and giving well-researched evidence to back up your opinion.

For example, take the essay question:
Why did the National Party win the 1948 election?
In this essay, you are not meant to simply list the reasons why the National Party won the election. There are many different reasons and interpretations as to why the Nationalists won the election. You need to state which reasons you believe are the most important. You also need to justify your choice.

Step 1: Identify the reasons for the Nationalist victory
Make a list of the reasons why the Nationalists won the 1948 election.
These could include the following:

Whites were terrified of the rapid rate of African urbanization.

Smuts had failed to deal effectively with post-war problems such as housing shortages and rising costs.

African farm labourers left the farms for new jobs in the city. As a result, there was a labour shortage and many white farmers switched their support from the United Party to the National Party.

According to the Sauer Report, racial segregation was the only way of dealing with the problem.

Afrikaner nationalism had become a strong force in South African politics.

Electoral **constituencies** were 'weighted'. Rural constituencies (where most Afrikaner nationalists lived) had more MPs than did urban constituencies (where most SAP supporters lived), even though fewer white voters lived in rural areas than in towns and cities.

... Developing essay writing skills: analysing the essay question (continued)

Step 2: Ask questions of each explanation
You need to consider the strengths and weaknesses of each explanation. To do this, you need to ask questions about each explanation. Let's consider the issue of African urbanization as an example:
– What evidence is there to suggest that African urbanization caused whites to vote for the National Party in 1948?
– How strong is this evidence?
– Does the explanation of African urbanization tell the whole story?
– Evaluate the strengths and weaknesses of this explanation.
Follow the same process for the other explanations that you have listed.

Step 3: Make a judgement
Based on the evidence and your evaluation of the strengths and weaknesses of each explanation, you should make a judgement as to which explanation is the most important.

Activity 5: Writing a history essay (*)

GRADE 11: LO 2, AS 2; LO 3, AS 2 and 3

Now that you have done an analysis of the question, write the essay, using the guidelines outlined above.

Why did the National Party win the 1948 election?

Note: Not all the information you need for writing this essay appears in this book. You need to consult your history textbooks, notes and other sources in order to write a comprehensive essay on this question.

GRADE 9
Content: What was apartheid and how did it affect people's lives?

GRADE 11
Content: How did apartheid entrench ideas of race?

THE IMPLEMENTATION OF APARTHEID

Once the National Party was in power, it began to pass a wide range of apartheid laws. These laws aimed to ensure racial separation in all aspects of social life and to control the movement and economic activity of blacks.

PROHIBITION OF MIXED MARRIAGES ACT, NO 55 OF 1949	SUPPRESSION OF COMMUNISM ACT, NO 44 OF 1950
IMMORALITY AMENDMENT ACT, NO 21 OF 1950	PREVENTION OF ILLEGAL SQUATTING ACT, NO 47 OF 1953
POPULATION REGISTRATION ACT, NO 30 OF 1950	BANTU EDUCATION ACT, NO 47 OF 1953
GROUP AREAS ACT, NO 41 OF 1950	RESERVATION OF SEPARATE AMENITIES ACT, NO 49 OF 1953

▲ *All 148 apartheid laws are listed in this way on a wall in the Apartheid Museum.*

New words

sombre – solemn and sad
absurdity – something unreasonable and ridiculous

When one looks at the long list of apartheid laws that dominates a wall in the Apartheid Museum, it is a **sombre** reminder of just how many laws were passed to ensure the separation of the races. In this book, we look at some of these laws and the impact that they had on the lives of ordinary black South Africans.

The Prohibition of Mixed Marriages Act, No 55 of 1949
This law prohibited marriage between whites and people of other races.

The Immorality Amendment Act, No 21 of 1950
Sexual relations between black and white South Africans were forbidden. To enforce this Act, police raided houses and broke into bedrooms to photograph couples breaking the law. The Apartheid Museum has recorded the way in which the police harassed one particular couple, Professor Blacking and Dr Desai.

◀ *Mr de Wet, the magistrate in this case, peering through a bedroom window to check whether the police could actually have seen Professor Blacking and Dr Desai having sex.*

▶ *Professor Blacking and Dr Desai were forced to emigrate to Britain, after being found guilty under the Immorality Act. Others were not so lucky, and spent time in prison.*

The Population Registration Act, No 30 of 1950
This law classified every South African according to their particular racial group. This would determine where they were allowed to live and what work they could do. This law had a terrible effect on people whose racial identity was not clear.

For example, families could suddenly find themselves divided. Parents who were classified as African might be told that their children had been classified as coloured. Their children had to go and live in a so-called coloured area, while the parents had to live in an area reserved for Africans.

In an attempt to maintain racial purity, officials used a variety of strange tests to determine whether a person was white, coloured, African or Indian. As you enter the separate entrances to the Apartheid Museum, you can see a number of sources on racial classification. These sources highlight the sheer **absurdity** of the methods used by the government to classify people into different races.

▶ *Adapted from* Apartheid: The Lighter Side *by B. Maclennan, Chameleon Press, Cape Town, 1990, p. 20.*

Source A
Mr W.H. Stuart, the Native Representative for the Transkei, claimed to have a highly scientific method of determining a person's racial category:

The eyelid test is this: when a person closes his eyelid under ordinary conditions the colour is continuous and uniform, there is nothing to indicate coloured blood. But if the eyelid is rather startlingly white that is one of the signs.
I used to test people by dropping something and their eyes would look downwards – and then you knew who they were. It was so simple.

Source B

The Star

February 1980

1979 had at least 150 'chameleons'

Political staff

PARLIAMENT – More than 150 people officially changed colour last year.

They were reclassified from one race group to another by the stroke of a government pen.

The Minister of the Interior, Alwyn Schlebusch, answered a question in Parliament today on the number of racial classifications that took place in 1979.

- A total of one hundred and one coloured people became white.
- One Chinese became white.

- Two whites received coloured classification.
- Six whites became Chinese.
- Two whites became Indians.
- Ten coloured people became Indians.
- Ten Malays became Indians.
- Eleven Indians became coloured.
- Four Indians became Malays.
- Three coloured people became Chinese.
- Two Chinese were reclassified as coloured.
- No blacks became white and no whites became black.

Activity 6: Analysing a variety of sources

GRADE 9: LO 1, AS 3
GRADE 11: LO 1, AS 3

1. Look at Source A. What method did W.H. Stuart use to determine someone's race?
2. The 'eyelid test' comes from a book called *Apartheid: The Lighter Side*. This suggests that this source is amusing. Do you find it funny or not? Give reasons for your answer.
3. Explain the meaning of the headline in Source B. (∗)
4. How do you think it was possible for so many people to be reclassified into different racial groups in 1979? (∗)
5. Why do you think the Nationalist government thought it was necessary to classify people along racial lines? (∗)
6. What do you think were the effects on the lives of people who were reclassified in terms of the Population Registration Act? (∗)

Prevention of Illegal Squatting Act, No 52 of 1951

One way of dealing with 'swamping' in towns was to build large townships like Soweto, far from the white suburbs. At the same time, new migrants were prevented from coming to live permanently in the towns through tight influx control measures, such as passes and police checks.

The Group Areas Act, No 41 of 1950

The Group Areas Act enforced residential segregation. Towns and cities were divided into areas, each reserved for one race only. All blacks living in so-called 'white' areas were forcibly removed to new areas, set aside solely for black occupation.

Sophiatown was a freehold African township near the centre of Johannesburg. It was declared a 'white' area under the Group Areas Act. District Six, an area in the middle of Cape Town with a mixed race population, was also declared a 'white' area under this Act. Thousands of black people were forcibly removed from both these areas, causing enormous heartache and incalculable loss.

Source A

Mrs Gadija Jacobs, a former resident, talks about how it felt to be removed from District Six in the 1970's:

Oooo, don't talk about the Group Areas Act, please don't talk about it to me. I will cry all over again. There's when the trouble started ... When they chucked us out of Cape Town. My whole life came changed! What they took away they can never give back to us! It won't never be the same again ... I cannot explain how it was when I moved out of Cape Town and I came to Manenberg ... Oooo my God, my whole life was tumbling down! I couldn't see my life in this raw township! You know, far away from family. All the neighbours were strangers. That was the hardest part of my life, believe me ... They destroyed us, they made our children ruffians.

▲ *In the 1950s, the vibrant freehold township of Sophiatown was destroyed. The removal trucks arrived early in the morning and took the residents to Meadowlands in Soweto. In its place, a new white suburb was built. It was called Triomf – triumph!*

The Bantu Education Act, No 47 of 1953

This Act was meant to provide mass education to Africans. One purpose was to take the ***tsotsis*** off the streets and discipline them. Another was to train Africans to do unskilled labour.

The Natives will be taught from childhood to realize that equality with Europeans is not for them. There is no place for the **Bantu** child above the level of certain forms of labour.

◄ *In 1953, Dr H.F. Verwoerd, who was the Minister of Native Affairs at the time, declared that African education should be inferior to that of other races and that Africans should be educated only far enough for them to be useful labourers.*

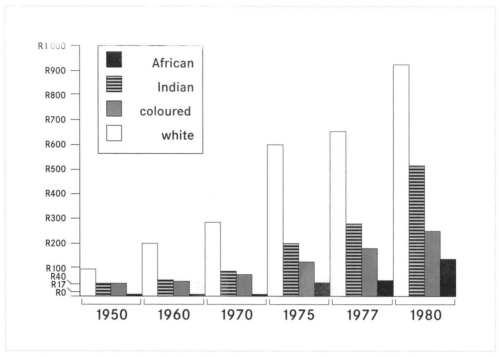

▲ *Per capita spending on education from 1950 to 1980.*

Activity 7: Analysing a graph of government spending on education

GRADE 9: LO 1, AS 3
GRADE 11: LO 3, AS 1

1. Which population group received the least money for education in the years 1950 to 1980?
2. 'Per capita' means per head or per person. In 1960, how much did the government spend on education per pupil if the pupil was white; African; coloured or Indian?
3. What does this graph tell you about trends in government spending on education from 1950 to 1980?
4. What does this graph and Verwoerd's quote tell you about the government's attitude towards education for Africans in South Africa? Provide evidence from these sources to back up your answer. (∗)
5. Why did the government have this attitude towards African education? (∗)
6. What do you think the impact of the government's unequal spending on education for different races has been on development in South Africa? (∗)

The Reservation of Separate Amenities Act, No 49 of 1953

Black and white people were forced by law to use separate public facilities, such as parks, beaches, entrances to buildings, post offices, buses and public toilets. In theory, these facilities were meant to be equal but in practice they hardly ever were. This policy caused a great deal of anger amongst the majority of South Africans. This was racism with a very public face, and it was experienced on a daily basis.

 Skills development: how to analyse cartoons

A cartoon is a drawing that makes a particular point, often by using humour or **satire**. A political cartoon usually highlights an absurdity or makes fun of or criticizes a personality or issue that is currently in the news.

Step 1: Place the cartoon in its historical context

Identify the event that the cartoon is about. The following questions will help you to do this.

- To what historical event does the cartoon refer?
- When did the event take place? (The date of the cartoon will help you to answer this question.)
- Where was the cartoon published?

Step 2: Identify and explain important elements in the cartoon, such as:

- The people in the cartoon, and who they represent
- Any symbols or objects which may appear in the cartoon
- The action that is shown in the cartoon
- The caption of the cartoon, if there is one.

Step 3: Identify the message of the cartoon

To do this, you need to look at the cartoonist's use of humour.

It is important to remember that a cartoonist usually makes fun of or criticizes an issue. A cartoon is not a neutral or objective representation of an issue.

Activity 8: Analysing a political cartoon

Analyse the cartoon below by answering these questions. To do so, follow the four steps outlined in the skills section on *How to analyse a cartoon*.

GRADE 9: LO 1, AS 2
GRADE 11: LO 1, AS 4

▲ *Cartoon by Abe Berry, 1966.*

1. What event or issue inspired the cartoon?
2. What period of history does the cartoon reflect?
3. Who are the people in the cartoon? Who or what do they represent?
4. What other elements are there in the cartoon, and how do they aid our understanding?
5. What is the message of this cartoon? (★)
6. How has Abe Berry used humour to get this message across? (★)

The Natives Abolition of Passes and Co-ordination of Documents Act of 1952
The movement of Africans into so-called white areas was strictly controlled through the pass laws. Under this new law, all previous permits and passes were combined into a single reference book – the *dompas* – which all African men had to carry. In 1956, African women were also forced to carry passes

GRADE 9
Content: What was apartheid and how did it affect people's lives?

GRADE 11
Content: How did apartheid entrench ideas of race?

THE PHOTOGRAPHS OF ERNEST COLE

One of the installations in the Apartheid Museum is a photographic exhibition of the work of Ernest Cole, a black photographer who told the story of the hardships and **humiliation** of blacks living under apartheid in the 1960s. After experiencing police harassment, Cole went into exile. His photographs were published in America in his book *House of Bondage* which was immediately banned in apartheid South Africa.

While the outside world was fortunate enough to see some of his powerful images, this exhibition at the Apartheid Museum provides South Africans with the first opportunity to see his work.

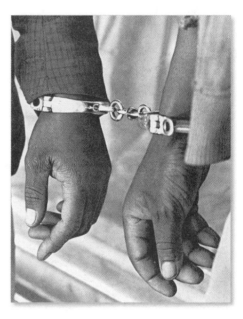

▲ *Ernest Cole tried to convey the harshness of the pass laws, both through his photographs and his words. He said: "In 1964, some 2 200 000 crimes were reported in South Africa. One third of these were not crimes in any moral sense, but crimes that only a black person could commit – by being in the wrong place, at the wrong time, with the wrong papers."*

◄ *This photograph of miners undergoing a medical examination highlights the horrors of the migrant labour system. Ernest Cole captures the humiliating experience of adult men, standing naked, and being subjected to inspection, rather like cattle at an auction.*

▲ *When a forced removal took place, the residents were ordered out of their homes, their belongings piled on the pavements, and the bulldozers moved in, destroying the township within minutes. Ernest Cole himself experienced the pain of forced removal.*

◄ *An infant suffering from advanced malnutrition. Like one in every four African children in South Africa in the 1960s, he died before his first birthday. Apartheid created an unequal society, in which most Africans lived lives of poverty and hardship.*

New words

humiliation – injuring the dignity and pride of somebody

lens – in this instance, it means a camera. A lens is the part of the camera through which the photographer focuses on the section of the image to be photographed.

Activity 9: Designing an exhibition poster

GRADE 9: LO 1, AS 2
GRADE 11: LO 3, AS 4

Imagine that the Apartheid Museum is holding an exhibition of photographs called "Apartheid through the **lens**". You have been invited by the Apartheid Museum to design a poster to advertise this exhibition. Your poster should contain the name of the exhibition and a single photographic image, which you think powerfully captures the meaning and impact of apartheid.

1. Design the poster for the photographic exhibition.
   What photograph would you use for the poster? If you are unable to make a copy of the photograph, you may describe the photograph that you would use. You may choose any photograph from this book or any other suitable photograph you can find.
2. Write a few lines to explain and justify why you have chosen this particular photograph for your poster.

GRADE 9
Content: Divide and rule: the role of the homelands

GRADE 11
Content: How far was apartheid in South Africa part of neo-colonialism in the post World War Two world?
Content: How did apartheid entrench ideas of race?

THE CREATION OF THE BANTUSTANS

Dr H.F. Verwoerd was the prime minister of South Africa from 1958 until 1966, when he was assassinated. Verwoerd was responsible for further refining the policy of apartheid into what he called 'separate development'.

In 1959, the Promotion of Bantu Self-Government Act was passed. According to this law, the reserves which had been created through the 1913 Land Act, would become separate 'countries' known as homelands or Bantustans. Every African in South Africa would become a 'citizen' of one of these homelands.

Each homeland would have its own government, which supposedly gave Africans full political rights. In the homelands, Africans would be able to develop separately and independently from whites. Ten separate homelands were established, each based on the African language spoken in the area.

Why did the government introduce Separate Development?

At the heart of the issue were the political rights of Africans and the question of democracy. The white government wanted to convince the world that South Africa was a democracy in which everyone had the right to vote. They explained that Africans would have the right to vote for their own political leaders in their homelands, but would have no political rights in South Africa.

By dividing Africans into ten different cultural, political and ethnic groups, the Nationalist government could claim that there was no African majority living in South Africa. Moreover, by highlighting the ethnic identities of Africans, the government hoped to create divisions among them and prevent the growth of a united African nationalism that could threaten the apartheid state.

The homelands were meant to become politically and economically independent. In truth, they never were. The former reserves were underdeveloped, with mostly infertile soil and no industries. People were unable to make a living in the homelands, and many had to work as migrant labourers in the cities of South Africa.

Forced removals

The government began to force the black people who lived in so-called 'white' rural areas to move into the homelands. Their land was taken away from them and sold to white farmers at very low prices. Forced removals was one of the most shocking and inhumane aspects of the apartheid system. Between 1960 and 1994 over three and a half million people were deliberately uprooted from their homes and their livelihoods, and plunged into poverty and hopelessness in the barren Bantustans.

Source A

In their homelands there are measureless and limitless opportunities for the Bantu.

◀ *M.C. Botha, Minister of Bantu Affairs and Administration in the 1960s.*

Source B

The township of Schmidtsdrift, near Kimberley, housed 7 000 Africans in territory that had been legally set aside for Africans. But it was in the middle of European land, so in 1968 officials and police loaded most of the Africans into lorries and drove them away to an African reserve near Kuruman on the edge of the Kalahari Desert. The area was totally unsuitable for crops or grazing because of its low rainfall. People arrived in the area looking fairly fit, but were soon starving. Several hundred died.

▲ *Adapted from* Divide and Rule: Race Relations in South Africa 1938-1977, *R. Childs, MacMillan, 1990, p. 59.*

Source C

◀ *This is a resettlement area in the Ciskei. The only facilities that the government provided were toilets.*

Activity 10: Analysing a map

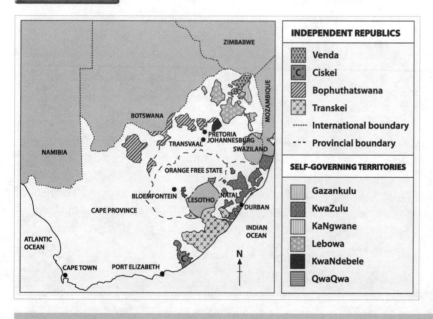

GRADE 9: LO 1, AS 3
GRADE 11: LO 1, AS 3

1. Identify the names of the ten different homelands and where each was located.
2. In which homelands do you think the Tswana people, the Zulu people and the Ndebele people lived?
3. Why do you think the government created the homelands along ethnic lines? (∗)
4. Nearly all the homelands were far away from the major urban areas in South Africa. What do you think the impact of this was? (∗)
5. Do you think that the Nationalist government succeeded in turning South Africa into an 'all-white' country by creating the homelands? Explain your answer. (∗)

CHAPTER 4

RESISTANCE TO APARTHEID

MAYIBUYE! ¡AFRIKA!
- The ANC Youth League

NON-VIOLENT PROTEST IN THE 1950s
- "Open the jail doors, we want to enter!":
  The Defiance Campaign
  - Repressive government legislation and actions
- "The People shall govern": The Freedom Charter
- The Treason Trial
- "Strijdom, you have struck a rock!":
  Women's resistance

THE 1960s – THE ROAD TO ARMED STRUGGLE
- The formation of the PAC
- The Sharpeville Massacre
  - What really happened at Sharpeville? Dealing with
    conflicting sources
- Moving towards the armed struggle
- The Rivonia Trial

THE 1970s – THE YOUTH TAKE CHARGE
- Steve Biko and the Rise of Black Consciousness
- The death of Steve Biko

THE SOWETO UPRISING OF 1976

GRADE 9
Content: Repression and resistance to apartheid

GRADE 11
Content: What was the nature of resistance to apartheid?

MAYIBUYE! ¡AFRIKA!

From the 1940s to the 1970s, resistance to apartheid took many different forms. In the 1940s, the resistance movement was still **moderate**, but in the 1950s, it turned to open, but non-violent, confrontation. In the early 1960s it took up arms in the struggle. The state met every attempt at resistance by increasing its repression.

Despite the South African government's harsh policies and the growing poverty and hardship of the African people, there was little organized black resistance against the state until things began to change in the 1940s. There were many popular struggles during this time, including housing protests and bus boycotts. Many of these struggles were inspired by the activities of the Communist Party of South Africa (CPSA), which was formed in 1921. A large number of the leaders of the CPSA were white.

▲ *Members of the Communist Party of South Africa helped organize lifts for the residents of Alexandra during the bus boycotts of 1943.*

The ANC Youth League

The African National Congress (ANC) remained out of touch with the mood and needs of most Africans. It was only when the ANC Youth League was formed in 1944 that the ANC began to adopt a more mass-based approach.

Youth Leaguers such as Anton Lembede, its first president, Nelson Mandela, Oliver Tambo and Walter Sisulu called for a **militant** programme of action, based on mass protests, boycotts and passive resistance. The Programme of Action was only adopted by the ANC in 1949 when the Youth Leaguers began to play a prominent role and the movement dedicated itself to mass action.

▶ *Anton Lembede, the first president of the ANC Youth League.*

Source A
Interview with Joe Matthews of the ANC Youth League

We no longer want to go on deputations to the government. The Xuma* idea of going off to Cape Town to see a minister every time there was a crisis must come to an end. And we must have strikes, and mass action.
Carter and Karis, Reel 12A

* Dr Xuma became the president of the ANC in 1940. He was most concerned with the organization of the ANC and did much to make its running more efficient.

Source B
David Bopape, a Youth Leaguer, criticized the ANC

The ANC recruited the top-level type of people so that our conferences were mainly attended by what we regarded as intellectuals. The ANC didn't go down enough, to the masses.

Activity 1: Analysing different sources to gain understanding

1. What is Joe Matthews' main criticism of the ANC in Source A?
2. In Source B, what is David Bopape's view of the ANC leadership in the 1940s?
3. What is similar in these two criticisms of the ANC? (*)
4. Using these two sources and your own knowledge, explain why the Youth League was critical of the ANC in the 1940s. (*)

GRADE 9: LO 1, AS 3
GRADE 11: LO 1, AS 3

NON-VIOLENT PROTEST IN THE 1950s

GRADE 9
Content: Repression and resistance to apartheid in the 1950s

GRADE 11
Content: What was the nature of resistance to apartheid?

Throughout the 1950s, there were many campaigns and protests against apartheid and the apartheid laws. There was a **groundswell** of resistance as people responded in overwhelming numbers to calls for **civil disobedience** and defiance throughout the country.

In this section, we will look at some of the most important campaigns. Most acts of resistance during this time were intended to be non-violent, though they did become violent from time to time, usually as a result of brutal police action.

◀ *A group of Indians, whites, coloureds and Africans defy the creation of separate facilities in the 1950s during the Defiance Campaign.*

New words

abolish – put an end to or get rid of

curfew – time at night after which black people were not allowed outside their houses and had to remain indoors until the next day

"Open the jail doors, we want to enter!": The Defiance Campaign

In 1952 the African National Congress launched the Defiance Campaign. A programme of civil disobedience was planned. This meant that large groups of Africans would peacefully but deliberately break the law. They aimed to get arrested and flood the country's prisons. They hoped that this would draw public attention to the apartheid laws and force the government to **abolish** them.

Mass rallies were held throughout the country and groups of volunteers were sent to break the law. They walked through 'whites only' entrances, sat in parks set aside for whites only, broke the **curfew**, and refused to carry their passes. As a result, over 8 000 people were arrested. The campaign had an enormous impact on people and ANC membership swelled from 7 000 to 100 000. However, the police responded with extreme violence, especially in the Eastern Cape. The state imposed heavy fines and even jail sentences, and the ANC was forced to call off the campaign.

Songs of resistance

As people were jailed, songs of struggle and resistance like Somlandela *were sung.*

Somlandela

Somlandela Luthuli	*We shall follow Luthuli*
Luthuli	*Luthuli*
Yonke indawo	*We shall follow him everywhere*
Lapo ayakona somlandela	*he goes*
Lelijele licwele uyalandelwa	*The jails are full, they show that we struggle for our freedom*

◄ *Albert Luthuli was the president of the ANC in 1952. He was the first South African to be awarded the Nobel Prize for Peace. Here he accepts the award in Oslo, Norway, in 1961.*

Music has played such a role that I just don't see how one would have pulled through the many years of struggle at home, in exile, in camps, all over the world, without being sustained by song.

◀ *Baleka Mbete, speaker of parliament.*

At no time has the liberation movement not been singing. At no time has the liberation movement not been dancing. Everywhere, culture becomes a very central and a very important element in this act of rebellion, in this act of assertion that we are human.

▲ *From the CD cover* Notes of SA Freedom Songs, *Mayibuye Centre.*

▶ *Thabo Mbeki, President of South Africa.*

Activity 2: Understanding the role of music in the struggle

1. In the context of the Defiance Campaign, what do you think the song *Somlandela* is trying to show?
2. How do you think a song like this would have helped people who were jailed during the Defiance Campaign?
3. Using the comments by Baleka Mbete and President Thabo Mbeki, as well as your own feelings, explain why music was an important part of the struggle.
4. Once you have finished working through this book, choose one of the resistance campaigns and write your own freedom song for it.

GRADE 9: LO 1, AS 3 and 5
GRADE 11: LO 1, AS 3; LO 3, AS 4

New words

disbanded – closed itself down, discontinued as a political party

state of emergency – a period during which the government suspended the rule of law and took special powers to rule the country. The police and army could arrest anyone they believed to be a threat to the state

banning orders – a government order or decree which led to a person being banned. This was usually imposed on a person for a period of five years.

Repressive government legislation and actions

The Suppression of Communism Act of 1950 made the Communist Party illegal and gave the government the power to declare any similar organization illegal as well. The Communist Party **disbanded** itself just before this legislation became law.

The Public Safety Act of 1953 enabled the government to declare a **state of emergency** if it believed that public order was threatened.

The government also placed **banning orders** on political activists. A banned person was restricted to his/her district, had to report to the police twice a day, could not be in the company of more than one person, and could not be quoted. This effectively silenced many activists. Organizations could also be banned, which meant they ceased to exist.

"The People shall govern": The Freedom Charter

In the 1950s, different groups within the liberation movement came together to form the Congress Alliance. The Alliance included the ANC, the South African Indian Congress, the South African Congress of Democrats (an organization of whites opposed to apartheid), the Coloured People's Organization and the South African Council of Trade Unions.

The Alliance started the Congress of the People Campaign. Volunteers travelled throughout South Africa to collect the demands of ordinary South Africans for a just and free society. These demands were listed in the Freedom Charter, which was presented to the Congress of the People in Kliptown in 1955. You can see video footage of this event in the Apartheid Museum.

The Congress of the People Campaign was important because it mobilized people over a lengthy period and so helped to revive the ANC. The ANC formulated a programme for the Congress Alliance which would guide it for the next forty years.

THE FREEDOM CHARTER
We, the people of South Africa, declare for all our country and the world to know:

That South Africa belongs to all who live in it, black and white, and that no government can justly claim authority unless it is based on the will of the people.

The people shall govern.
All national groups shall have equal rights.
The people shall share in the nation's wealth.
The land shall be shared by those who work it.
All shall be equal before the law.
All shall enjoy equal human rights.
There shall be work and security for all.
The doors of learning and culture shall be opened.
There shall be houses, security and comfort.
There shall be peace and friendship.

▲ The opening words and main clauses of the Freedom Charter.

Activity 3: Analysing the Freedom Charter

GRADE 9: LO 1, AS 3 and 5
GRADE 11: LO 1, AS 3; LO 3, AS 4

1. Find and write down the different demands from the Freedom Charter which show what the people wanted: democracy; redistribution of land and wealth; an end to apartheid; freedom; a just society.
2. Which of the Freedom Charter's demands do you think is the most important? Explain why you think so.
3. Which of the Freedom Charter's demands do you think have been met today in the new South Africa? Provide evidence to support your answer. (*)
4. Choose one of the demands of the Freedom Charter, and design your own poster for it.

◀ *Posters were an important form of protest, particularly in the 1980s. They often provided a unifying symbol for a particular struggle or movement. The Apartheid Museum has dedicated a whole wall to struggle posters.*

This poster was produced by the democratic movement in 1985 to celebrate the 30th anniversary of the Freedom Charter. It shows that in the 1980s the Freedom Charter was still a powerful liberation symbol. Many of the principles of our South African Constitution were inspired by the demands of the Freedom Charter.

The Treason Trial

The South African government regarded the Freedom Charter as a **treasonable** document and it claimed that the Congress Alliance was plotting to overthrow the state. As a result, 156 members of the Congress Alliance were arrested and charged with **treason**. The treason trial lasted from 1956 to 1961, but the government failed to prove that treason had been intended and so everyone was eventually **acquitted**.

You can see this very famous and interesting photograph in the Apartheid Museum. It is interesting because it has been constructed. The photographer, Eli Weinberg, had received permission to photograph all 156 trialists in Joubert Park, Johannesburg. However, when the park superintendent found out that most of the people were black, he withdrew permission. So Weinberg set up benches outside the park and photographed the people in different groups. He then put the groups together in a single photograph.

GRADE 9: LO 1, AS 2
GRADE 11: LO 1, AS 4

Activity 4: Analysing a photograph

1. Does the fact that you know that this photograph was constructed affect its meaning in any way? Explain.
2. Does the fact that it was constructed affect your appreciation of it in any way? Explain.
3. In what way does this photograph help us to understand this period of history? (∗)

"Strijdom, you have struck a rock!": Women's resistance

Partly because African women experienced fewer restrictions than men, they were at the forefront of resistance in the 1940s and the early 1950s.

In the 1950s the government tried to extend its control over the African women who were moving to the cities and to restrict their freedom when they got there. To achieve this, it planned to extend the pass system to include women. For several years women resisted this attempt.

By 1956 their resistance had grown into a national movement. It reached its climax on 9 August 1956 when 20 000 women marched to the Union Buildings in Pretoria and handed over letters of protest against the proposed pass laws to Prime Minister J.G. Strijdom.

The women's resistance failed to achieve its objectives and the pass laws were extended to apply to African women in the late 1950s. Today, 9 August is a public holiday on which we celebrate National Women's Day, remembering the role played by women in defying the unjust pass laws, as well as the strength and courage of women in South Africa as a whole.

▲ *Raheema Moosa, Lilian Ngoyi, the president of the ANC Women's League and the non-racial Federation of South African Women, together with Helen Joseph and Sophie Williams, led the women's march to Pretoria in 1956.*

GRADE 9
Content: Repression and the armed struggle in the 1960s

GRADE 11
Content: What was the nature of resistance to apartheid?

THE 1960s – THE ROAD TO ARMED STRUGGLE

The formation of the PAC

In 1959 a group within the ANC, led by Robert Sobukwe, P.K. Leballo and Zeph Mothopeng, broke away and formed a new organization called the Pan Africanist Congress (PAC). As Africanists, they were opposed to working with organizations that were not African. They were particularly opposed to the Congress Alliance, which also included the white-based Congress of Democrats.

◀ Robert Sobukwe, the leader of the PAC, who was later imprisoned for six years on Robben Island and died in Kimberley as a banned person in 1978.

Interview with Robert Sobukwe, leader of the PAC, January 1959:

Question: *What are your differences with the ANC?*
Sobukwe: *We differ radically in our conception of the struggle. We firmly hold that we are oppressed as an African nation. To us, therefore, the struggle is a national struggle. There are those in the ANC who maintain, in the face of the hard facts of the SA situation, that ours is a class struggle ... We, however, stand for the complete overthrow of white domination.*
Question: *What is your answer to the accusation that you are anti-white?*
Sobukwe: *In South Africa then, once the white domination has been overthrown and the white man is no longer 'white-man boss' but an individual member of society, there will be no reason to hate him and he will not be hated by the masses. We are not anti-white, therefore. We do not hate the **European** because he is white! We hate him because he is an oppressor.*

▲ Quoted in Making History, *Grade 12 by J. Pape et al., p. 327.*

Activity 5: Analysing an oral source

1. What does Robert Sobukwe mean by "a national struggle"?
2. What do you understand by the term "class struggle"? Refer to Chapter 1 pages 12 and 13 on the Radical Approach to explaining apartheid to help you answer this. (★)
3. Why did Sobukwe break away from the ANC?
4. Do you think that Sobukwe's views are racist? Justify your answer. (★)

GRADE 9: LO 1, AS 3
GRADE 11: LO 1, AS 3

Activity 6: Debating a controversial issue (★)

Throughout this book there are a number of examples of whites, such as Helen Joseph and several of the Treason Trialists, who played an important role in the struggle against apartheid. Was Sobukwe's view that whites should not be part of the struggle correct? Debate this issue in class.

GRADE 9: LO 1, AS 4
GRADE 11: LO 3, AS 2

The Sharpeville Massacre

On 21 March 1960, the Pan Africanist Congress organized a protest against the pass laws. Still using the methods of non-violent protest, they planned to march to the local police station, hand in their passes and give themselves up for arrest. A large crowd gathered outside the police station at Sharpeville (near Vereeniging). The police fired on the crowd, killing 69 people and wounding 180 people.

What really happened at Sharpeville? Dealing with conflicting sources

When you analyse the following sources describing the events at Sharpeville, you will see that they do not agree with each other. In fact, they present conflicting views of what happened.

Source A
An historian's account

*At 1.15 p.m., with nearly 300 police facing a crowd of 5 000, a **scuffle** broke out at the gate leading into the police station. A police officer, accidentally or deliberately, was pushed over. The attention of the front rows was focused on the gate and they surged forward, pushed by people behind them who wanted to see what was happening.*
*At this stage, according to police witnesses, stones were thrown at them. The more inexperienced constables began firing their guns **spontaneously**. The majority of those killed or wounded were shot in the back. Altogether 69 people died, including eight women and ten children. 180 people were wounded.*

▲ *From T. Lodge,* Black politics in South Africa since 1945, *p. 210.*

Source B

▲ *The police fire on a retreating crowd at Sharpeville.*

Source C
An eyewitness account by journalist Humphrey Tyler

*When the shooting started it did not stop until there was no living thing in the huge compound in front of the police station. The police have claimed they were in desperate danger because the crowd was stoning them. Yet only three policemen were reported to have been hit by stones – and more than 200 Africans were shot down. The police also have said that the crowd was armed with '**ferocious** weapons', which littered the compound after they fled. I saw no weapons, although I looked very carefully, and afterwards studied the photographs of the death scene. While I was there I saw only shoes, hats and a few bicycles left among the bodies.*

Source D
Statement by the **South African High Commissioner** in London in 1960

According to the factual information now available, the disturbances at Sharpeville on Monday resulted from a planned demonstration of about 20 000 natives in which demonstrators attacked the police with assorted weapons including firearms. The demonstrators shot first, and the police were forced to fire in self-defence and avoid even more tragic results.

▲ *Sources C and D: Quoted in: R. Sieborger et al.,* What is Evidence?, *Francolin Publishers, 1996, p. 19.*

New words

scuffle – a confused or disorderly fight at close quarters

spontaneously – not planned or caused or suggested by outside influences or as a result of an order given by a superior

ferocious – fierce or savage

South African High Commissioner – the chief representative of the South African government in Britain

---

Activity 7:	Trying to establish the facts

Since these sources present conflicting or different points of view about what happened at Sharpeville, try to establish the facts by copying out and completing the following table:

GRADE 9: LO 1, AS 3
GRADE 11: LO 1, AS 2

Establishing the facts	Source A	Source B	Source C	Source D
What was the size of the crowd?				
Was the crowd armed and dangerous?				
Was the action planned?				
Were the police acting in self-defence?				

▲ *Adapted from* What is Evidence? *by R. Sieborger and G. Weldon, Francolin Publishers, 1996, p. 19.*

Reliability is as easy as ABC

Use the ABC method to work out whether or not a source is reliable.

A is for Author: Who is the author or creator of the source? Would this make the source trustworthy? For example, an eyewitness account may be trustworthy because the person witnessed the actual events. On the other hand, an eyewitness may be too involved in the events to give a balanced view. A secondary source produced by an historian may be reliable because the historian has worked with a wide range of sources. On the other hand, the historian may be biased and present sources that reflect only one point of view.

A is for Audience: For what audience did the writer intend the source? In other words, what was the writer's intention in producing the source?

B is for Bias: Is the source biased in any way? Does it give only one side of events? Does it use emotive language or make exaggerated comments to persuade you to react in a certain way? Or does it try to present a balanced point of view?

C is for Consistency: Do all the facts in the source support each other?

C is for Comparison: Is the information in the source backed up by similar information presented in other sources?

Activity 8: | **Determining the reliability of sources**

GRADE 9: LO 1, AS 2; LO 3, AS 1
GRADE 11: LO 1, AS 4

1. Explain what you see happening in Source B – the photograph on page 64.
2. How important is it that Source C on page 65 was written by an eyewitness? (∗)
3. What do you think the intention of the writers of Source A (page 64) and Source D (page 65) are? How do their intentions differ? (∗)
4. Using the ABC for reliability provided above, work out whether Source A and Source D are reliable accounts of what happened at Sharpeville. (∗)
5. Using all the sources about Sharpeville and your own knowledge about it, do you think that the crowd at Sharpeville was armed and dangerous?
6. Imagine that you were a reporter at the time of the events at Sharpeville. Write a newspaper report, based on the knowledge you have gained from analysing the above sources and stating what you believe happened at Sharpeville.

Moving towards the armed struggle

Sharpeville marked a turning point in the anti-apartheid struggle. There was a massive outcry, both nationally and internationally, about police actions there. The government responded by declaring a state of emergency and banning the ANC and the PAC.

Both the ANC and the PAC had to rethink their strategies. They decided to embark on a policy of armed resistance. The ANC set up a military wing called *Umkhonto we Sizwe*, '*the Spear of the Nation*', also known as MK. The PAC established its military wing called Poqo, which means 'standing alone'. Both groups were prepared to use **sabotage** and violence to overthrow the government.

▲ Ruth Mompati represented the ANC during the first round of negotiations that led to democracy in South Africa.

Ruth Mompati, a long-standing ANC member, explains why the ANC turned to armed resistance.

"All the time that the African National Congress was using peaceful means to try to bring change in South Africa, the reaction from the regime was violent. People were shot at peaceful meetings. Thousands upon thousands of South Africans have died at the hands of the police ... There's also the violence of conditions of living in South Africa ... We decided that, if the gun is what the South African regime has used to rule us, it will have to be the gun that breaks that rule."

▲ *Quoted in* Lives of Courage: Women for a new South Africa *by D. Russell.*

◄ *This cartoon was published in* Punch, *a British magazine, in 1960. It portrays the ANC's decision to move towards armed struggle.*

Activity 9: Analysing a cartoon and an oral source (∗)

1. Study the above cartoon carefully. Explain what the following symbols in the cartoon stand for: the planting machine, the crop that is growing.
2. What does the cartoonist see as the major cause of the armed struggle?
3. What do you think the cartoonist's attitude is towards the armed struggle?
4. Why does Ruth Mompati believe that the ANC had no choice but to start using violence?
5. Using this cartoon, Ruth Mompati's evidence and your own knowledge, explain why the ANC decided to embark on an armed struggle.

GRADE 9: LO 1, AS 2; LO 2, AS 3
GRADE 11: LO 1, AS 4; LO 2, AS 3

New words

sabotage – illegal destruction of property or equipment by people who are opposed to the state

guerrilla warfare – small and often secret groups which fight the enemy by using unconventional methods, rather than through direct confrontation in a battle

The Rivonia Trial

Between 1961 and 1963, 200 acts of sabotage took place in South Africa, mostly organized by the ANC. In 1963 the headquarters of Umkhonto we Sizwe (MK), at Lilliesleaf Farm in Rivonia, was raided and the entire leadership of MK was arrested. They were charged with "recruiting people for training in sabotage and **guerrilla warfare** for the purpose of violent revolution".

Eight of the trialists (Nelson Mandela, Walter Sisulu, Govan Mbeki, Raymond Mhlaba, Dennis Goldberg, Ahmed Kathrada, Elias Motsoaledi and Andrew Mlangeni) were found guilty and sentenced to life imprisonment. Photographs of these men hang prominently in the Apartheid Museum. They show several of them in disguise because they were on the run. The Rivonia Trial and the imprisonment of the ANC leaders broke the power of MK and the ANC inside South Africa.

During the Rivonia Trial, Mandela made a four-hour address to the court, ending with these famous lines:

During my lifetime I have dedicated my life to this struggle of the African people. I have fought against white domination, and I have fought against black domination. I have cherished the idea of a democratic and free society in which all persons live together in harmony, and with equal opportunities. It is an ideal which I hope to live for and to achieve. But, if needs be, it is an ideal for which I am prepared to die.

THE 1970s – THE YOUTH TAKE CHARGE

Steve Biko and the Rise of Black Consciousness

The early 1960s saw the end of effective opposition from the ANC and PAC within South Africa. *Umkhonto we Sizwe* and *Poqo* had been effectively crushed and the key leaders were either banned, jailed or in exile. In the 1970s, however, black resistance took on a new form – black consciousness. Black consciousness (BC) started in South Africa in 1969 as a university student movement led by Steve Biko.

Biko was a medical student who was born in East London in 1946. While he was studying, he formed SASO, the South African Students Organization, and became its first president. SASO was a breakaway movement from NUSAS (National Union of South African Students), a mainly white student movement that was opposed to apartheid. Biko believed that a white-led organization could not fight for the interests of black students.

The main ideas of black consciousness were:
• pride in being black
• a determination that blacks should end their dependence on whites.

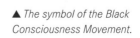

▲ *The symbol of the Black Consciousness Movement.*

Blacks think that everything good is white. This attitude comes from childhood. When we go to school, our school is not the same as the white school ... This is part of the roots of the feeling of being inferior that our kids get as they grow up. Our homes are different, the streets are different. So you begin to feel that there is something incomplete about being black, and that completeness goes with being white.

When you say 'Black is beautiful' ... you are saying, man, you are OK as you are, begin to look upon yourself as a human being.
Adapted from I Write What I Like *by Steve Biko.*

▲ *Steve Biko, the father of the Black Consciousness Movement.*

The death of Steve Biko

The tragic story of Steve Biko is told in the Apartheid Museum's Hall of Political Executions. As Steve Biko became more popular, the government increasingly saw him as a threat. He was banned in 1973 and detained without trial for a few months in 1976. In 1977 he was arrested again. He was kept in a cell, naked and in chains. He was severely tortured by the security police. Within 18 days of his arrest, he was dead. He was only 30 years old.

The Apartheid Museum has a video recording of the **callous** reaction of the Minister of Justice at the time, Mr Jimmy Kruger, to the death of Steve Biko.

▲ *The Hall of Political Executions in the Apartheid Museum.*

New word

callous – showing a lack of feeling for somebody else's pain or hardship

On the night of 12 September 1977, Mr Biko was found dead in his cell. I never at any stage said what Mr Biko died of. I don't know what he died of ... his death leaves me cold!

◀ *Jimmy Kruger, Minister of Justice.*

The ideas of BC caught on particularly among the youth and they formed many organizations in support of BC. In 1972 the Black People's Convention (BPC) was formed to co-ordinate all BC activities. Some historians believe that the ideas of black consciousness influenced the actions of the students in the Soweto Uprising in 1976 which is described on page 71. Others disagree.

I do not remember any liberation movement, such as the Black Consciousness Movement or the South African Student Movement (SASM) contributing to our daily meetings and discussions. In short, as students we faced our own destiny and problems.

▲ *Sifiso Ndlovu, a historian who was a student in Soweto in 1976.*

SKILLS **Developing essay writing skills: writing introductions**

The introduction is a very important part of an essay. It provides your reader with their first impression of your writing, and it is possible that it will influence their judgement of your essay.

The purpose of the introduction is to:
- identify the problem posed by the essay question
- outline how you are going to structure your argument in the essay.

Some useful phrases to use in an introduction:
- This essay will include …
- The purpose of this essay is to …
- I will argue that …

Below is an example of an introduction to the following essay question:

To what extent was the rise of black consciousness an important cause of the Soweto Uprising of 1976?

This essay will explore the role played by the ideas of black consciousness in influencing the actions of some student leaders in 1976. It will argue that, while the ideas of black consciousness were important, there were other more immediate causes of frustration which led to the uprising.

This essay would then go on to examine some of the issues that led to frustration, such as:
- The harsh conditions in the townships which the youth experienced every day
- The situation in schools, including the language policy of teaching half the subjects in Afrikaans
- The lack of employment opportunities for school leavers and the feelings of hopelessness that this caused.

Activity 10: **Writing an introduction for an essay (∗)**

GRADE 11: LO 2, AS 1 and 2
GRADE 12: LO 2, AS 1 and 2;
LO 3, AS 3

Write an introduction to the following essay topic, using the guidelines outlined above:

"Steve Biko had been harassed by police for years. They suspected he was a dangerous agitator trying to inspire the people to violent resistance."

Discuss the extent of Steve Biko's involvement in resistance during the 1970s.

THE SOWETO UPRISING OF 1976

In 1975 the Minister of Bantu Education, M.C. Botha, ordered that African schools must teach half of the subjects in Standards Five and Six (now Grades 7 and 8) in Afrikaans. People opposed this because they believed that the children's education would suffer. They also opposed it because they saw Afrikaans as the language of the oppressor.

On 16 June 1976, 20 000 students marched through Soweto in protest against the use of Afrikaans in schools. The police fired on the crowd. Hector Pieterson was the first child to die. He was 13 years old. The students responded violently and unrest swept throughout the country.

Although the uprising was eventually crushed by the police, it had important results. It was the single biggest challenge to the government and the apartheid system. The government could no longer ignore resistance. In many ways, the Soweto Uprising was a major turning point and marked the beginning of the end of apartheid.

SKILLS **Causation – long-term, short-term and immediate causes**

History is concerned with causation, i.e. explaining why things happened in the past. All historical events have causes. It is often possible to classify them into long-term, short-term and immediate causes.

- Long-term causes are the underlying conditions that create tension and build up over a period of time.
- A short-term cause is an event or issue that takes place shortly before the event takes place
- An immediate cause is an event or action that sparks off a series of events.

Read the following sources to help you understand why the Soweto Uprising took place.

Source A
Statistics for Soweto 1976

Population:	1.5 million
Area:	87 square kilometres
Location:	±10km south west of Johannesburg's city centre
Administration:	West Rand Administration Board
Electricity:	20 % of homes
Hot water:	5% of homes
Hospitals:	1
Schools:	280
Number of pupils per class:	60
Average rent per month:	R40 for a two-roomed house
Average income per month:	R100
Average cost of living per month:	R140
Number of homeless:	400 000
Employment:	very little in Soweto – most people commute daily to work elsewhere in the Greater Johannesburg region

▲ What is History? *Skotaville Educational Division, p. 45.*

1. If only 20% of homes had electricity, 5% of homes had hot water and there was only one hospital for 1.5 million people, what do these statistics tell us about the general living conditions in Soweto in 1976?
2. Look at the average income of people living in Soweto and compare it with their monthly expenses. What does this tell us about the living standards of the general population of Soweto?
3. Was there adequate schooling in Soweto? Use the statistics to prove your answer. (*)
4. Based on these statistics, if you lived in Soweto in 1976 what would your major **grievance** have been? (*)
5. How do these statistics help you to understand why there was such anger in the townships in 1976? (*)

Source B

Given black grievances ranging from low pay and poor housing to the pass laws and political repression, virtually any issue could have set off a generalised upheaval. The one that finally did was the regime's decision to implement a policy of teaching half the courses in African secondary schools in the southern Transvaal through the medium of Afrikaans.

▲ *E. Harsch,* White Rule – Black Revolt, *p. 35.*

Source C

◀ *Students marching in Soweto on 16 June 1976.*

Source D

No new secondary schools were built in Soweto between 1962 and 1971 because it was government policy that all new schools should be built exclusively in the homelands. As a result, secondary school classes were severely overcrowded and many teachers resorted to increasingly harsh methods to maintain control. Pupils bitterly resented this.

▲ *Adapted from* Soweto: A History *by P. Bonner and L. Segal, p. 78.*

Source E

*People who were trying to promote political awareness were encouraged when, early in 1973, SASO students staged walkouts from black universities. Many of these 'drop-outs' became teachers in Soweto schools. Armed with BC ideology, SASO activists inspired a new spirit of **radicalism**. Many students tell of the impact these teachers had on their lives.*

▲ *Adapted from* Soweto: A History *by P. Bonner and L. Segal, p. 80.*

Source F

There was 'an atmosphere of revolt' in the 1970s. There were the liberation struggles in Mozambique, Angola, Zimbabwe and Namibia. There were the black workers' strikes in the 1970s.

▲ *Quoted in* The Right to Learn *by P. Christie, p. 243.*

Source G

It affected us both positively and negatively. A lot of us missed out on normal school. But it assisted us to know that the struggle for freedom needed the commitment and support of the liberation movements who were then banned, as well as leaders who were imprisoned. It set in our lives the role of full-time activism. The Soweto uprising changed the history and landscape of the politics of the country permanently. Young people swelled the ranks of the liberation movements abroad, especially the ANC.

▲ *Baby Tyawa was a student who was involved in the Soweto Uprising. In the above interview in 2003, she explains the significance of the uprising.*

Activity 12: Identifying short-term, long-term and immediate causes

1. Sources A to F each emphasize a particular cause of the Soweto Uprising. Copy out and complete this table. Identify what each source states as the major cause of the Soweto Uprising. Then decide whether the cause is a long-term, short-term or immediate cause. Refer to the skills section on causation earlier in this chapter on page 71.

GRADE 9: LO 2, AS 2
GRADE 11 and 12: LO 1, AS 2 and 3

	Major cause of the Soweto Uprising	Long-term/short-term/immediate causes and reason for your choice
Source A		
Source B		
Source C etc.		

2. Which source do you believe provides the most convincing explanation for the outbreak of the Soweto Uprising? Provide a clear reason for your answer. (*)

CHAPTER 5

FROM APARTHEID TO DEMOCRACY

TOTAL STRATEGY
- Strengthening the army

'TOTAL STRATEGY' – REFORM
- Labour – Workers Unite!
- Making homelands 'independent'
- A permanent urban African population
- Creating a new African middle class
- The Tricameral Parliament
- The formation of the United Democratic Front
  – Political posters

TOTAL STRATEGY – REPRESSION
- Voices of detainees

RESISTANCE INTENSIFIES
- The role of the Churches
- White resistance and the End Conscription Campaign
- International pressure

THE MOVE TO DEMOCRACY
- Negotiations begin
- The first democratic elections

GRADE 9
Content: Repression and the growth of mass democratic movements in the 1970s and 1980s: external and internal pressure

GRADE 12
Content: How did South Africa emerge as a democracy from the crises of the 1990s?
- The crisis and collapse of apartheid

TOTAL STRATEGY

The Soweto Uprising of 1976 changed the political landscape of South Africa forever. Resistance intensified, international pressure against the government increased and the economy went into serious decline. The South African government began to feel increasingly threatened.

I'm giving you a final warning: one man, one vote in this country is out – that is never!

Quoted in South Africa since 1948 *by C. Culpin, p 109.*

◀ *In 1978, P.W. Botha succeeded B. J. Vorster as prime minister.*

New words

communist forces – the South African government considered anyone who opposed apartheid a 'communist'. In the context of the Cold War, talk about a 'communist threat' encouraged fear and rallied white support for the government.

onslaught – attack

reform – gradual changes to improve the political situation

P.W. Botha was determined to keep South Africa under white control. His government believed that white South Africa was under threat from **communist forces** both within and outside South Africa. He called this threat the 'total onslaught'. Botha's response to 'total **onslaught**' was 'total strategy'.

'Total strategy' aimed to fight the 'total onslaught' in two ways:
- The government gradually introduced a number of **reforms** in the hope of winning support in the black community.
- At the same time, it intensified its repression in order to stamp out all opposition.

Strengthening the army

An important aspect of P.W. Botha's 'total strategy' policy was to strengthen the position of the military. Before Botha became prime minister, he had been Minister of Defence. As prime minister, he increased the power of the army considerably. Two years of military service for all white men became compulsory and the constant presence of the army in the townships was a regular feature of the 1980s.

▶ *This Casspir, which dominates the 1980s exhibition in the Apartheid Museum, is a sinister symbol of the army's threatening role and widespread presence in the 1980s.*

GRADE 9: LO 1, AS 3
GRADE 12: LO 1, AS 3

The growth of military expenditure and personnel				
	1961	1974	1977	1981
Total military personnel	106 000	328 000	439 500	592 000
Military spending in millions	72	707	1 940	3 000

▲ *From IDAF., Apartheid: The Facts, 1983, p. 68.*

1. By how much did the South African government increase its military spending between 1974 and 1981?
2. In the period 1961 to 1981, how many more people were drawn into the armed forces?
3. Using the table and your own knowledge, explain what events in South African history may have persuaded the South African government to increase the size of its army and the amount it spent on the military: in 1961 and 1977?
4. How do you explain the sharp increase in the military budget as well as the numbers of military personnel from 1977 to 1981? (*)
5. Why did the apartheid government choose to use the army to implement its 'total strategy'? (*)

'TOTAL STRATEGY' – REFORM

GRADE 9

Content: Repression and the growth of mass democratic movements in the 1970s and 1980s: external and internal pressure

GRADE 12

Content: How did South Africa emerge as a democracy from the crises of the 1990s?
- The crisis and collapse of apartheid

As part of Botha's policy of reform, he made **concessions** in a number of different areas. He hoped that by doing this, many blacks would be **bought off** and would be satisfied with these so-called reforms. In this way, resistance would die down and whites would be able to hold on to power.

In this section, we look at some of the different reforms Botha's government introduced. These included the recognition of African trade unions, the granting of independence to some homelands, the recognition of a permanent urban African population, the attempt to create an African middle class and the creation of the **Tricameral Parliament**.

Labour – Workers Unite!

Under the umbrella of reform, the government recognized African trade unions in 1979. Until then, African trade unions had been legal but were not allowed to negotiate with employers over wages and working conditions.

Why did the government recognize African trade unions at this time? On the one hand, it was part of P.W. Botha's strategy of reform. But the government was also forced to respond to the growing **militancy** among workers. In 1973 nearly 60 000 workers embarked on a wave of strikes in Durban as a response to a sharp increase in food prices. The Durban strikes were a major turning point in the history of African trade unions. Inspired by the strikes, more and more African trade unions began to spring up and organize workers.

The recognition of African trade unions in 1979 made it easier for them to operate. They realized that they would have more power if they worked together. This led to the formation of the Federation of South African Trade Unions (FOSATU) and other umbrella bodies. FOSATU supported the principle of non-racialism and believed that all workers should unite and fight for better conditions.

New words

concessions – giving some rights as a result of pressure

bought off – won over by giving them a stake in the system

Tricameral Parliament – 'tri-' means three and '-cameral' means chamber. Therefore the Tricameral Parliament was a parliament with three separate chambers, in this case, the House of Assembly for whites, the House of Representatives for coloureds and the House of Delegates for Indians.

militancy – willingness to take aggressive and direct action

The push for unity continued and in 1985, FOSATU merged with other unions to form a new federation – the Congress of South African Trade Unions (COSATU). COSATU, with nearly half a million members, was the largest trade union organization ever formed in South Africa.

Under COSATU's banner, workers organized countless strikes and protests in the factories and on the mines to improve wages and working conditions. However, as repression intensified, COSATU was drawn more and more into the struggle for broad political change and became one of the most important anti-apartheid forces.

May Day – 1 May – is traditionally celebrated as Workers' Day throughout the world. COSATU often used May Day as a call to action for workers. After the 1994 elections, 1 May was recognized as Worker's Day in the new South Africa. Today we celebrate it as a public holiday and remember the struggles of working class people for their rights.

▲ *Poster produced in the Western Cape to celebrate the launch of COSATU. It is inspired by Soviet posters of workers in the USSR.*

Activity 2: **Analysing a political poster**

GRADE 9: LO 1, AS 2 and 3
GRADE 12: LO 1, AS 3 and 4

1. Look at the following symbols in the poster, and explain what they mean:
   – the red flag
   – the bright yellow sun
   – the hammer
   – the raised fists.
2. What does the slogan "One Country - One Federation" mean?
3. Using the poster and your own knowledge, explain why African trade unions wanted to create one federation.
4. Why do you think this poster was produced? (∗)
5. Do you think this is an effective poster? Explain your answer. (∗)

Making homelands 'independent'

The government decided to grant limited independence to four homelands. This would entitle them to their own president and give them some administrative powers. However, the homelands remained financially dependent on South Africa and did not have the right to make their own policies.

In this way, P.W. Botha and his cabinet hoped to create a group of African leaders in the homelands who depended on the South African government's support. In 1976, the Transkei became the first homeland to gain its 'independence', followed by Bophuthatswana and Venda in 1977 and the Ciskei in 1981.

Chief Mangosuthu Buthelezi refused to accept 'independence' for KwaZulu and massive resistance by the people in the remaining Bantustans eventually led the government to scrap its plans to extend 'independence' to them.

◄ Most people considered Kaiser Matanzima, the leader of the Transkei, and other homeland rulers as puppets of the white South African government. He was nevertheless given an official funeral in post-apartheid South Africa.

A permanent urban African population

African people living in the urban areas remained a huge problem for the government, but it was eventually forced to recognize that there was a permanent urban African population outside of the Bantustans. From the late 1970s, plans were launched to develop African townships, in the hope that electricity, improved services and new housing would reduce militancy among residents.

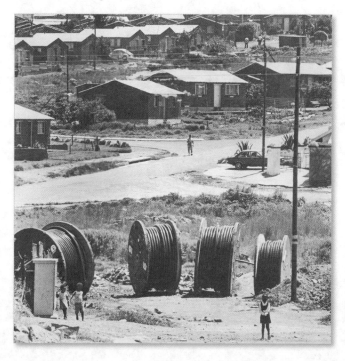

◄ From the late 1970s, people in Soweto were allowed to buy new houses rather than rent them, and new suburbs for the better-off were constructed in Diepkloof Extension, Orlando West and Selection Park.

Creating a new African middle class

At the same time the state tried to create an African middle class which would have an economic stake in the system and so be loyal to the government. Many measures were introduced, both economic and cultural, to encourage better-off urban Africans to adopt a middle class lifestyle. Separate amenities legislation was relaxed to allow middle class blacks access to hotels, cinemas and restaurants in white areas.

The film about the 1980s in the Apartheid Museum begins by showing the government's drive to create better housing for some residents in Soweto.

The Tricameral Parliament

In 1983, P.W. Botha introduced a new **constitution** for South Africa, which gave limited parliamentary representation to coloureds and Indians. There was to be a new **parliament**, the Tricameral Parliament. The new constitution allowed coloureds and Indians to vote for their own representatives who would sit in their own chambers of parliament. Africans were still denied the right to vote. Their interests would be represented by black, local or community councils.

The white, coloured and Indian chambers each handled laws that related to their 'own affairs'. This meant that issues relating to education, health and community affairs were dealt with separately by each chamber. For example, the House of Representatives – the coloured chamber of parliament – would make decisions about coloured education.

All matters that related to the wider issues of governing the country, such as defence, taxation, and industry were called 'general affairs'. The **cabinet**, which included representatives of all three chambers, made decisions on these. Under this new constitution, P.W. Botha became state president. He had far greater powers than any previous head of state, and could decide which matters were 'general' and which were 'own affairs'.

People saw the 1983 Constitution for the **sham** democracy that it was. Not only was the Tricameral Parliament racially segregated, but it excluded Africans altogether.

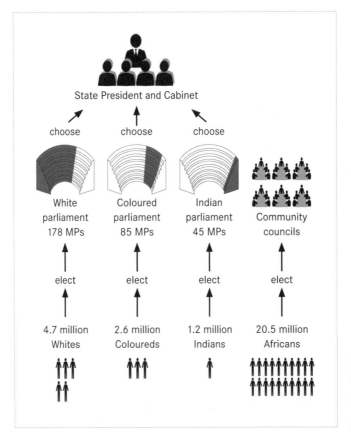

◀ A diagram showing how Botha's new Tricameral Parliament was supposed to work
C. Culpin, South Africa since 1948, p. 114.

1. How many members of parliament would represent the:
   - 4.7 million whites
   - 2.6 million coloureds
   - 1.2 million Indians?
2. How were the rights of the 20.5 million Africans to be represented:
   - at a local or community level?
   - at a national level?
3. According to the diagram, who was the highest power in the land?
4. Using the diagram and your own knowledge, explain what powers the Indian and coloured chambers of parliament would have in the new constitution.
5. According to the government, the Tricameral Parliament provided real power sharing in South Africa. To what extent was this true? (∗)

The formation of the United Democratic Front

Two **umbrella bodies** were formed in 1983 to oppose the new constitution – the National Forum, which took a black consciousness position, and the United Democratic Front (UDF) which was aligned to the ANC and supported the principle of non-racialism. A contest developed between the two groups and the UDF emerged as the stronger. The UDF eventually consisted of over 500 anti-apartheid organizations, which came together to oppose the Tricameral Parliament and the whole system of apartheid.

The UDF called for all coloureds and Indians to **boycott** the elections for the new parliament and for Africans to boycott elections for the local community councils. In 1984, only one in five black voters actually voted in the elections. The UDF campaign had successfully denied the new parliament any kind of **legitimacy**.

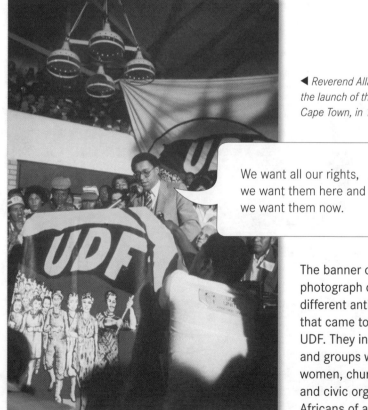

◀ *Reverend Allan Boesak, speaking at the launch of the UDF in Mitchells Plain, Cape Town, in 1983.*

We want all our rights, we want them here and we want them now.

The banner of the UDF in the photograph on the left shows the different anti-apartheid groups that came together to form the UDF. They included trade unions and groups which represented women, churches, students, youth and civic organizations and South Africans of all races.

New words

umbrella bodies – large organizations which co-ordinate smaller organizations under their influence

boycott – the practice of refusing to participate in a particular activity in order to show opposition to it

legitimacy – recognition and acceptance by society

Political posters

In the 1980s, political posters became an important form of protest. Most of these posters were produced by grassroots community structures around the country and addressed all forms of inequality in apartheid South Africa. By producing their own posters, these organizations were demanding their right to be heard and communicating their opposition to apartheid. The Apartheid Museum has dedicated a whole wall to these political posters.

◀ *Posters like this were produced to appeal to coloureds and Indians not to vote in the 1984 elections for the Tricameral Parliament.*
Source: Images of Defiance, *SAHA.*

Activity 4:   Working with two sources on a theme

GRADE 9: LO 1, AS 2
GRADE 12: LO 1, AS 4

◀ *This cartoon by Abe Berry was published in the City Press in the late 1980s. It shows how PW Botha's reforms left Africans feeling that these were empty promises.*
Source: A. Berry, Act by Act, *p. 94.*

▶ *A UDF poster, indicating what really lay behind P.W. Botha's reforms.*

1. What does the size of the package in the cartoon say about the reforms that P.W. Botha introduced?
2. What do you think the caption means, "Never mind the small package – just look how large I've spelt it out for you!"?
3. What point is the poster making about the nature of Botha's reforms?
4. How does it make this point?
5. In what ways do the cartoon and poster make a similar comment about the nature of Botha's reforms? Explain your answer. (*)
6. Do you agree with the ideas presented in the cartoon and poster? Provide evidence to back up your answer. (*)